essential educat

THE 6 ANCHORS
OF STUDENT RETENTION

PROVEN STRATEGIES FOR LONG-TERM STUDENT SUCCESS & ENGAGEMENT IN ADULT EDUCATION

The 6 Anchors of Student Retention: Proven Strategies for Long-Term Student Success & Engagement in Adult Education

ISBN 978-1-940532-56-1

For more information, contact:
Essential Education Corporation
895 NW Grant Avenue
Corvallis, OR 97330
phone: (800) 931-8069

Essential Education provides innovative, effective HSE test preparation and adult learning programs centered on the learner's needs.
For more information, please visit http://www.essentialed.com/educators/.

TABLE OF CONTENTS

RETENTION ANCHOR 3
CREATING CULTURE: FOSTERING AN ENVIRONMENT FOR STUDENT SUCCESS 43

RETENTION ANCHOR 4
GETTING CONNECTED: CREATING RELATIONSHIPS FOR CONTINUANCE 81

RETENTION ANCHOR 5

MEASURING PROGRESS: TRACKING, IMPROVING, & CELEBRATING GAINS

RETENTION ANCHOR 6

GROWING PROFESSIONALLY: CONTINUING EDUCATION FOR PROGRAM RETENTION

RESOURCES 147

APPENDIX 153

INTRODUCTION

Student retention is the heartbreak of adult education. Passionate teachers and program administrators work tirelessly to keep students enrolled and engaged. They devote time, resources, and an exhaustive amount of energy to encourage students to stay in class and on track for success. But the realities of adult student life pose a challenge to steady educational progress.

A robust curriculum and dynamic instruction are vital, but time is required for growth. The formula is simple. Students must stay in programs long enough to make meaningful progress. While consistent classroom attendance is challenging for all learners, adult students face unique barriers. Daily responsibilities, negative school experiences, and a lack of academic resources are very real obstacles for many adult students. When learning is inconsistent, growth is stifled, and motivation dwindles. Students become stuck in the revolving door of adult education. We know there's a problem, so what's the solution?

Essential Education focuses on identifying and addressing the challenges that impact adult learning. But this problem is a big one! Adult student retention is complex and nuanced. There is no magic pill or quick fix. Tackling this particular issue would call for more than a few educators and researchers to explore potential remedies. It would require large-scale collaboration. We would need to dig in, hypothesize, test, and analyze multiple strategies in a variety of classroom environments. We would need to ask really good questions and have our answers challenged. We would need to try, fail, evaluate, and try again. We needed a team. So we turned to you, adult educators, for support.

In partnership with the Coalition of Adult Basic Education (COABE), we invited select teachers and administrators from across the nation to join Essential Education's **Professional Learning Community (PLC)** to closely examine six retention-impacting factors. Appropriately called "Retention Anchors," these crucial elements focus on collaborative findings and emerging research within the adult education community. The PLC reflections and activities within this guide will provide engaging strategies to utilize in any adult education classroom.

This guide will illuminate the unique characteristics, values, and needs of adult learners. It will explore what it means to create intentional, timely, relevant, and engaging instruction. The topics will examine classroom culture, strategies to support student motivation, personalized learning, and success skills. The research will highlight the connection between relationship and retention and propose activities to strengthen this link. Student assessment practices will move educators beyond reviewing numbers on a page to measuring, tracking, and celebrating student progress. This guide will be your resource and springboard for educator collaboration and continued professional development.

As we explore each Retention Anchor, we'll synthesize current data, note problems to address, and analyze each factor's impact on adult education classes and programs. We'll provide teachers and administrators with evaluatory tools and practical resources to implement robust and positive change.

With the PLC as our anchor, we'll highlight the experiments, insights, and success stories of hardworking teachers and administrators striving toward a common goal. Join us on our journey to explore, discover, and share real solutions for adult student retention. ***Let go the anchors!***

Why Retention "Anchors"

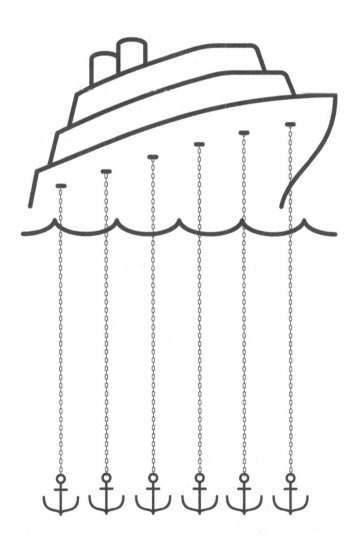

Before we begin, let's create a mental picture of what it looks like to "anchor" retention. Imagine program retention is a ship. To be successful, the ship must be well made, in proper working order, and on schedule for continual maintenance. This "retention ship" must consider program structure, curriculum, scheduling, and resources, as these facets hold everything together and keep the program "afloat." But when the retention ship pulls into the harbor to evaluate continuance and measure student progress, educators must consider a different set of factors: the Retention Anchors.

What really impacts student attendance and program completion? Which elements address barriers to student participation and growth? What are the crucial aspects of a thriving adult education program? Are those essential aspects balanced? Are those facets working together or against each other?

Successful Adult Program Retention

In looking at the contributing factors of successful adult program retention, six primary indicators stand above the rest. These are the **Retention Anchors** addressed in this guide:

KNOWING YOUR AUDIENCE: WHO IS THE ADULT STUDENT?

CAPITALIZING ON THE NOW: APPLYING JUST-IN-TIME LEARNING

CREATING CULTURE: FOSTERING AN ENVIRONMENT FOR STUDENT SUCCESS

GETTING CONNECTED: CREATING RELATIONSHIPS FOR CONTINUANCE

MEASURING PROGRESS: TRACKING, IMPROVING, AND CELEBRATING GAINS

GROWING PROFESSIONALLY: CONTINUING EDUCATION FOR PROGRAM RETENTION

As we examine these foundational factors, remember that each of these Retention Anchors is equally significant. They must work together to be truly effective. Just as a physical vessel could become unstable during a storm with only one anchor, our programs must balance each factor to maintain stability and guide student progress. For instance, educators may understand their students' needs and interests, but if instruction is not tailored to utilize this information, learning suffers. Teachers may build welcoming and engaging classrooms, but students will miss growth opportunities if they are not armed with tools to measure and track their own progress. To weather the storm and keep students on course, program retention must adapt and respond accordingly.

Just as adult students cannot be taught through a one-size-fits-all approach, program retention cannot be addressed with a single solution. This guide will provide a means to examine each of the six Retention Anchors in detail while giving reflection tools to measure individual educator and program performance. It will also provide resources to help link these elements and create a balanced and structurally sound path to student continuance.

RETENTION ANCHOR 1 /

KNOWING YOUR AUDIENCE

WHO IS THE ADULT STUDENT?

REVIEWING THE RESEARCH

Do You Know Your Students?

Think deeply about your response before you answer.

Do you know what they value and fear? What experiences have shaped their current circumstances? Do you know where they have been, where they want to go, and what obstacles stand in their way?

Intentionally educating adult learners and facilitating a path to success rests just as much, if not more, in *who* students are as in *what* they know. We must consider the demographics of the adult learning community before we begin a meaningful discussion about student retention.

"Demographic data can help provide a basis for understanding communities as they are now, where they've been, and where they're headed. It can be a powerful tool for tracking change over time and for uncovering the needs or strengths of a community to guide planning, policy development or decision making."

—Dan Veroff, University of Wisconsin—Madison

What Do We Know About Adult Learners?

As we explore the answer to this question, we will note generational distinctions within seven key characteristics of adult students. We will examine how each quality manifests itself in individuals characterized as Generation Z (Gen Z), currently 11–26 years of age, and students over 30 years of age comprised of Millennials, Generation X-ers, and Baby Boomers. We will provide a targeted focus on Gen Z. This generation already accounts for a significant portion of the adult learning community and will represent the majority of students in adult education programs within the next five to ten years. The following are seven key characteristics.

 Adult learners are diverse. They encompass various ages, backgrounds, values, and goals. Their experiences within the traditional school system can range from indifferent and distant to restrictive and painful. Differences in culture, learning style, and depth of knowledge combine to form one collective classroom.

Gen Z students expand this diversity further. The ever-changing shifts in values and priorities within this generation can challenge adult educators attempting to meet evolving student needs. Generational differences also exist among students within the 30+ age range; however, these distinctions tend to be more constant than those of Gen Z.

 Adult learners are busy. They try to balance career, family, and financial demands while maintaining social, emotional, and physical health. Finding additional time for study and knowing how to prioritize educational endeavors can be a challenge.

Life obligations and other demands for attention also differ between generations. For instance, Gen Z students tend to battle greater degrees of mental clutter. Technology and social media bombard them with constant messaging. Emerging generation expert Tim Elmore notes these students are "exposed to ten thousand messages daily when you consider posts, ads, TV shows, emails, videos, signs, and conversations in person." Students 30 and over are just as busy but experience more traditional demands as they juggle family, life, and financial responsibilities. There is simply too much to do and seemingly not enough time to do it!

 Adult learners tap into personal experience. This characteristic is one of the adult student's most significant benefits. Lifelong learning is grounded in real-world practice. Applying relatable knowledge and problem-solving skills can boost long-term memory and solidify understanding.

Gen Z and students over 30 may tap into differing degrees or types of life experiences, but the need for practical application exists across generations. Adult education classrooms flourish when instruction recognizes and integrates prior experience and personal interests. Student engagement soars when lessons and activities are relevant to their daily lives.

 Adult learners are uniquely motivated. Until you know a student's "why," you'll never get to their "how." What prompted your students to enter an adult education program? What keeps them going? What motivates them to push through barriers? These personal "whys" are shaped by countless factors as diverse as the students themselves. But getting to the heart of deeply rooted motivation is invaluable. A student's reason for seeking further education fuels the internal endurance and resilience needed to push through difficult circumstances. When someone's "why" is strong enough, they will endure any "how."

Students over 30 often cite immediate practical needs as their motivation for pursuing education. Two of the most common reasons are providing for a family and getting a better-paying job. Gen Z students have other ambitions. While they naturally care about meeting their day-to-day needs and building a stronger financial future, they don't tend to embrace traditional success norms. Many view themselves as advocates, often rejecting the status quo and seeking a path that promotes personal empowerment and societal change. Astute educators get to the core of their students' unique aspirations to keep them on track and engaged.

 Adult learners enjoy control over their learning. Accountability and investments of time, money, and resources are of greater significance when someone has autonomy over their learning. Adult students build confidence by choosing when and how they learn. Personal choice can be a powerful catalyst for educational buy-in.

With the power of personal choice in mind, we must address an increasingly frequent question. What teaching style do students prefer? Do students learn best with a "guide on the side" or a "sage on the stage"? The guide is a facilitator, pointing out key information and encouraging students to explore and dig deeper. The guide allows for free time and plans periodic check-ins. On the other hand, the sage is a disseminator of robust amounts of information, an expert in the field who tells and then asks the students to show. Before we proceed, let's do an activity.

Are You a Guide or Are You a Sage?

Think about the following aspects of instruction and use the scales below to note where you tend to land when teaching specific subject matter. Would you consider yourself more of a guide or a sage in these areas? For instance, if you spend significant time lecturing students in language arts, you may lean more toward being a sage. If you integrate group projects and peer collaboration in math, you may see yourself as a guide. Do some personal reflection below.

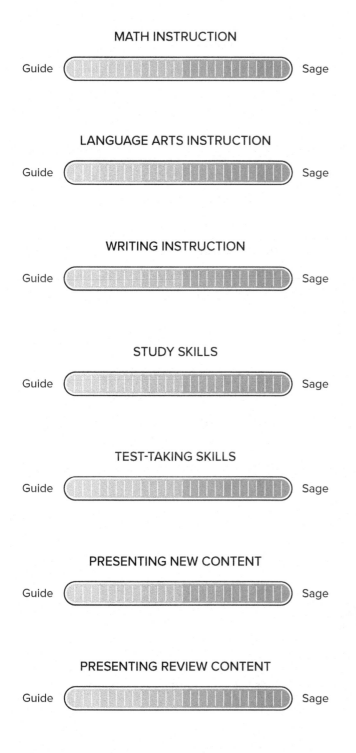

As you reflect on these areas of instruction, remember there is no right or wrong methodology. Pete Scales (2019) provides this valuable wisdom for educators in his appropriately named article, "'Sage on the Stage' or 'Guide on the Side.'" He writes, "Good teachers do not live exclusively at one end or the other; they can, as necessity requires, be either or both and most of the time will occupy the ground between the two" (Scales, 2019). In other words, adult educators must remain attuned and responsive to their students' needs and motivators.

Our Gen Z students collectively prefer a guide but often crave a sage when challenged or faced with difficulty. This particular generation wants to be seen as trailblazers and agents of change. They press toward their goals headlong but get stuck when encountering problems outside their scope. They need mentorship.

For students over 30, gaining autonomy in their learning allows them to address some of their unique motivations. For example, if a student's primary goal is to find a new or better job, allowing them to choose career-specific reading content or essay prompts gives them purposeful control over what they learn. In making this choice, learners may benefit from activities that speak to their "why" while ensuring they build the skills they need to reach their goals.

Adult learners are results-oriented. Does practice make perfect? Not necessarily. But practice does make progress. Adults must see that their efforts are paying off—the sooner, the better! Progress, even in its smallest amount, is still progress. Learners thrive when growth is valued and celebrated. The dilemma is that many students base success solely on performance.

The statement "If I didn't pass, I failed" is rarely true. They may not have hit the ultimate mark, but when there is growth, there is no failure. Both Gen Z students and those over 30 need help embracing this truth. Assisting adult students of all ages in setting small, measurable goals is foundational to personal success. Equipping students with tools to track effort and progress is vital to achievement.

 Adult learning is slower but deeper. This trait is tricky as it pushes against the adult learners' desire to see immediate results. Students often become frustrated when they view their progress as slow or unproductive. However, building the long-term memory and critical thinking skills required for high school equivalency completion or career development is rarely a quick process. When instructors champion the value of progress (no matter how slow) over perfect performance, learning is no longer measured in time but comprehension. Valuing meaningful growth over speed allows adult learners the time needed to solidify primary skills and take on more challenging content.

This "slower but deeper" characteristic can greatly encourage adult students when framed in a positive light. Students 30 and over need reminders that their effort to refresh and strengthen basic skills is an investment that will pay off when asked to tackle more complex problems. Gen Z students need reminders that a faster solution, the "hack," so to speak, rarely builds the foundational skills required for growth. Adult students may need more upfront learning, but the mature brain is primed for long-term understanding.

While demographic data is beneficial, we must avoid generalizations. It's easy to place all adult students into one category and neglect to see them as individuals. Arming ourselves with knowledge of the student base we serve is valuable, but focusing on each learner as an individual is critical.

EVALUATION AND REFLECTION

After introducing the importance of adult student demographics to the PLC, Essential Education proposed a challenge to the group. Each member was asked to choose one of the seven key characteristics of adult learners and set up an experiment to better understand or utilize that attribute in their classrooms. They then examined the trait through the targeted lens of retention and noted how tapping into the chosen characteristic could impact program stop gaps. The following experiments may inspire your research or encourage you to explore similar inquiries.

South Bay Adult School Experiment

Bilquis Ahmed of South Bay Adult School in Redondo Beach, California, decided to learn more about the busy lives of adult learners. She created a classroom chart (see Appendix A) to mark attendance and students' reasons for missing class over one month. Ahmed used emojis to represent common barriers, including work, transportation, childcare, appointments, illness, and personal circumstances (Figure 1.1). When students missed a session, they would indicate a reason and add it to the chart.

Within this particular class, Ahmed discovered work was the principal reason for absences. Due to numerous responsibilities, jobs often take priority over school. One student pointed out, "I have to eat and support my family. I have asked my supervisor not to schedule me during school

hours. However, it cannot be helped sometimes." Conflicting appointments, lack of childcare, and transportation issues were also key reasons for missing class.

Ahmed's research activity was valuable in several ways. It gave her insight into the lives of her students and provided an extra dose of empathy for the obstacles they encountered. For instance, she learned that many students try to schedule appointments outside of class time but often have to "take what they can get" due to conflicts with critical responsibilities like work and family.

The activity also allowed the class to share openly and find commonalities amongst themselves. Shared experiences are powerful and can positively enhance the dynamic of a diverse classroom. Acknowledging trouble spots allowed the class to brainstorm solutions to common obstacles, such as carpooling and a babysitting exchange to fight frequent transportation and childcare barriers.

Through this experiment, Ahmed gained significant insight into attendance within her class and can now identify and attempt to support specific patterns with individual students.

COMMON REASONS FOR ABSENCE
(over one month)

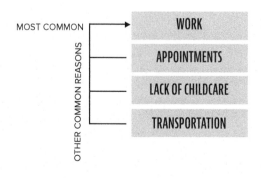

Figure 1.1 – General commonalities for missing class.

"Having a visual reminder of their attendance motivated the students. The students regularly sign in on a sheet turned into the office. [But] this large chart displayed predominantly on the wall helped students see what affects attendance for themselves and their classmates. It was a great way to learn about the barriers students face in attending and that students take great measures to avoid absences. The chart opened up conversations about how life intervenes and how absences affect progress in the class and towards goals such as finishing the ESL class to enroll in the GED program."

—Bilquis Ahmed, South Bay Adult School

Retention Anchor 1: Knowing Your Audience

Santa Cruz County Experiment

Nikki Andruschak Neal of Santa Cruz County Continuing Education chose to examine the desire for adult students to have control over their learning. She set out to discover if allowing students to select a specific topic of study versus a teacher-chosen topic would improve student attendance.

Neal teaches two classes. She assigned a specific subject and correlated assignments for the first class. The second class, however, was prompted to select an area of study and follow-up activities as a group. The second class, currently preparing for the GED social studies exam, opted to focus on history and government. Neal also asked each student to submit three additional ideas for lesson topics.

She made the following observation after the experiment: "Giving adult learners control over their learning sustained their attendance, which could also have an impact on student retention. Moreover, I witnessed my students tapping into their diverse personal experiences to complete assignments during this experiment. The students were uniquely motivated and went beyond the [chosen] tasks." Neal further noted increased group participation as students gained a stronger sense of control and inclusion.

"A majority of my students have English as their second language. I feel that having the opportunity to talk through the tasks with others helped them better understand concepts by seeing other viewpoints. I watched [them] feed off each other's excitement and ideas, building relationships in the classroom."

—Nikki Andruschak Neal,
Santa Cruz County Continuing Education

Briya Public Charter School Experiment

Lyle Ring, Lead ELL Teacher with Briya Public Charter School in Washington, D.C., opted to investigate the unique motivations of his adult students. First, he conducted extensive andragogical research to explore the science of teaching adults. He then analyzed the distinct differences between intrinsic and extrinsic motivation. Lastly, Ring set out to collect specific data on his students' motivational triggers. He created an online survey for anonymous student responses (see Appendix B).

After analyzing the results, Ring noted, "The survey shows that family has a primarily positive role in motivating students to stay in classes. All but one respondent indicated they agree or strongly agreed that their family motivates them to take and stay in classes. It also seems that having a student services team, on-site childcare, and technology has played a role in keeping students enrolled in the program."

Quick Reflection

Do you think family connections play a significant role in the lives of your students? If so, what are you doing to support this factor? Brainstorm a few ideas to strengthen this element and involve families in your program.

"[M]any students indicated that a better future for their children was a motivating factor for them. In conjunction with student services, this indicates that these parts of the program positively affect retention rates."

—Lyle Ring, Briya Public Charter School

ACTIVITIES AND APPLICATIONS

Now that you've learned about the common characteristics of adult learners and gained insight from fellow adult educators, it's time to apply what you've learned. Consider using the **Student Survey** (see Appendix C) to uncover demographic details specific to students and your classroom community. Post-survey, reflect on the data you collected and then work through the **Educator Evaluation** provided below.

Educator Evaluation

Do your students have common feelings about success and learning?

Do your students have common barriers to attendance?

Do your students have common goals?

Educator Evaluation (cont.)

Do your students have common motivating factors? Were there any surprising findings?

What are your top survey takeaways?

How can you use these takeaways to influence classroom management and instruction?

TOP TAKEAWAYS

Knowing Your Audience: Who is the Adult Student?

- **Adult learners are diverse.** They encompass various ages, backgrounds, values, and goals.

- **Adult learners are busy.** They try to balance career, family, and financial demands while maintaining social, emotional, and physical health.

- **Adult learners tap into personal experience.** This characteristic is one of the adult student's most significant benefits.

- **Adult learners are uniquely motivated.** Until you know a student's "why," you'll never get to their "how."

- **Adult learners enjoy control over their learning.** Accountability and investments of time, money, and resources are of greater significance when someone has autonomy over their learning.

- **Adult learners are results-oriented.** Learners thrive when growth is measured, valued, and celebrated.

- **Adult learning is slower but deeper.** Valuing meaningful growth over speed allows adult learners the time needed to solidify primary skills and take on more challenging content.

ANCHOR CONNECTION

Exploring Retention Anchor 1 has reinforced that knowledge is indeed powerful. Our diverse, uniquely motivated adult students seek meaningful results for deeply personal reasons. This understanding can be a crucial catalyst for improved program structure and classroom instruction.

But how exactly does this demographic knowledge influence retention? Knowing our students better isn't enough. We must intentionally put this information to work in concert with the other Retention Anchors yet to be explored.

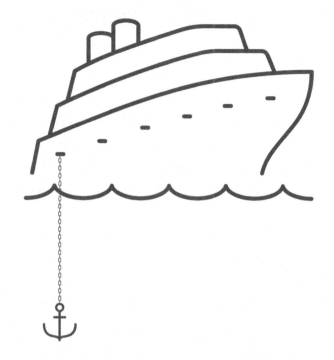

Use the following questions to note potential connections between understanding student demographics and supporting retention factors.

How can knowing your students impact your ability to create timely and relevant instruction?

How can knowing your students foster an environment for student success?

How can knowing your students help to enhance student and class relationships?

How can knowing your students aid in measuring student progress?

How can knowing your students facilitate professional development?

We will continue to ask these questions as this guide progresses. During each upcoming Retention Anchor, take time to stop and reflect on the insights gained within each topic and consider how the elements work together to support student continuance.

SUPPORT FROM ESSENTIAL EDUCATION

Essential Education products, programs, and services are expertly designed with students and educators in mind. Our efforts currently address key student characteristics in the following ways:

Adult learners are diverse. The student-facing resources of Essential Education seek to meet learners where they are in both academic level and depth of experience. Our content is intentionally inclusive. Instructional videos feature characters of varying races, ages, and backgrounds and support the needs of students with learning differences or difficulties.

Adult learners are busy. Essential Education's online learning platform is mobile-friendly to accommodate students on the go. Interactive workbooks include smartphone features via Virtual Tutor to enhance instruction in and out of the classroom.

Adult learners tap into personal experience. All Essential Education offerings are highly contextualized. Many high school equivalency subject units include "workplace connections" for practical life application and the development of transferable skills.

Adult learners are uniquely motivated. With tools to aid personal goal setting, Essential Education supports educators' deep understanding of their students. Robust reporting features in the student HomeRoom dashboard and the teacher Learning Management System (LMS) create a terrific framework for discussions about individual student success markers.

Adult learners enjoy control over their learning. Within the Essential Education platform, educators can work with each student to customize a plan that meets their needs. Our platform offers educators multiple ways to empower students to have greater autonomy over their learning while meeting required program standards.

Adult learners are results-oriented. Essential Education takes the guesswork out of adult learning. From tools to monitor and track study time to relevant measures of progress, students and teachers are given immediate feedback. Educator reports supply teachers with valuable insights into how to assist students in re-evaluation and continued improvement.

Adult learning is slower but deeper. With ample opportunities to review and refresh content, Essential Education creates an academic well from which students can continuously draw. Our adaptive learning programs are intuitive and responsive to the unique instructional needs of adult learners.

RETENTION ANCHOR 2/
CAPITALIZING ON
THE NOW
APPLYING JUST-IN-TIME LEARNING

REVIEWING THE RESEARCH

What Will You Teach?

We've explored the "who," now it's time for the "what."

What lessons and engagement strategies will you utilize? What will you do to meet a diverse group of learners where they are right now? What will you do to create experiences that encourage student attendance? Enter the practice of Just-In-Time Learning.

The Just-In-Time Learning concept, or JITL, has become increasingly popular in recent years. JITL refers to the idea that people learn most effectively when they can access the information they need when they need it, rather than being required to learn in a more traditional, "just in case" manner. Instead of storing information with the hope that it might be useful in the future, the JITL model seeks to target specific learner needs and encourages immediate application.

The origins of Just in Time Learning can be traced back to the manufacturing industry, where the concept was first introduced to improve efficiency and reduce waste in production processes. Manufacturers could increase productivity and save money by reducing inventory and producing goods only as needed.

The idea of applying JITL principles to education emerged in the 1990s. With the rise of the internet, it became feasible for people to access vast amounts of information on virtually any topic, anywhere in the world, at any time. But is real-time access to information all that is needed to learn? Simply acquiring information is useless without tools to help synthesize and make connections. Adult educators have the opportunity to facilitate student success by helping learners move beyond information collection to information application. Passing an exam is not a full indicator of growth. Outside of test scores, skills gains, and certificate completion, how do we know if our students are making strides toward success? To answer that query, we must revisit the manufacturing roots of JITL and ask another pivotal question: What are we producing?

How Will You Tailor What You Teach?

The demographic research explored in Retention Anchor 1 (Figure 2.1) is clear. The adult student population is diverse and representative of a myriad of ages, stages, aims, desires, and deeply personal "right now" requirements. There cannot be a universal answer to our question. We must make our response adaptable to individual student needs and goals. We must invoke a more open-ended reply that accounts for the varied objectives of each learner.

The PLC worked as a team to home in on a more versatile response. What are we producing? **People capable of taking their next step.** This statement may sound broad, but it accurately encompasses the personalized objectives of each student. One student's next step might be understanding a given subject, while another hopes to gain a specific skill, complete their high school education, or find and keep a better job.

ADULT STUDENT POPULATION
(2023 PLC research)

Figure 2.1 – Adult learner demographic research.

The possibilities are innumerable. These next steps differ because the people taking those steps differ. Without understanding the "who," we cannot create the "what."

Defining student success in this manner hits the core of JITL: personal learning and application. In embracing this model, wise educators consider **three attributes** when planning instruction.

 Immediate – Instruction that engages students in the moment.

 Predictive – Instruction that anticipates what is needed and when it will be needed.

 Targeted – Instruction that aims to address a distinct learning gap.

These key attributes form a foundation for contextualized learning and encourage the use of real-world examples and scenarios. Timely, practical application has been proven to be more motivating and meaningful than abstract theory. Just-In-Time Learning strategies lead to personal realizations that help students better understand a concept or develop a skill. When instruction is intentional and personally applicable, it sets the stage for "Aha!" moments.

The connection between Just-In-Time Learning and the "Aha!" moment is significant and rooted in neurological research. Scientists from Goldsmiths, University of London, led by Professor Joydeep Bhattacharya and Professor Christian Windischberger of the Medical University of Vienna, used functional Magnetic Resonance Imaging (fMRI) to study what happens in the human brain when individuals work to solve complex problems (Wilton, 2018). The study involved monitoring the neurological scans of adult volunteers. Participants were asked to solve 48 word puzzles and press a button as soon as they felt confident about their answers. They were instructed to indicate the exact moment they solved the problem. The researchers discovered that as the subjects found each answer, a deeper part of the brain that produces dopamine "lit up," leading to a "light bulb" of creative thought: the "Aha!" moment.

In the aptly titled article "Aha! Moments Linked to Dopamine Producing Regions in the Brain," Bhattacharya says, "For the first time, we have shown that the hub of the brain's reward system, the nucleus accumbens, 'lit up' with increased activation both when problems were solved and when people reported a strong 'Aha!' experience. The nucleus accumbens is part of a network activated when we experience pleasure or reward, and dopamine facilitates communication between this network and other brain regions involved with critical functions like emotion, memory, and attention. These findings may reflect the sudden 'jump' to a solution accompanied by a moment of intense relief, ease, or joy" (Wilton, 2018).

When adult learners solve problems and fill skill gaps directly connected to their personal priorities and objectives, the "Aha!" moment is even more powerful. An epiphany's connection to a specific next step leads the learner to a confident realization: "This really does matter! I will actually use this!" When students quickly apply what they've learned, they are more likely to take pride in their accomplishments, knowing their actions directly impact their lives. Excitement and motivation soar. Capitalizing on "the now," Just-In-Time Learning methods can transform adult education classrooms by encouraging flexible instruction relevant to students' immediate needs and current interests.

EVALUATION AND REFLECTION

Let's investigate Just-in-Time Learning by exploring a pivotal question: How do you prime the adult brain for an "Aha!" moment? We posed this query to the PLC and asked each member to create and evaluate a JITL activity to invoke an "Aha!" experience. As one might imagine, the educators' findings were as unique and diverse as the students they teach. However, the group's collective research and experimentation found several commonalities among effective methods to ready the brain for Just-In-Time Learning.

Classroom Mood and Excitement

PLC researchers first noted the mood of the classroom as foundational for student growth. Many discussed the aforementioned neurological data regarding the section of the brain shown to "light up" just before an "Aha!" moment. As this section of the brain is activated, dopamine is released, creating an experience similar to that felt in moments of excitement or happiness.

"When students enter a classroom with a calm and welcoming space, they are more likely to learn and seek opportunities to have control of their own learning."

—Iris McDuffie, CoreCivic

"Improving the mood of the class can be done before any instruction takes place or as a warm-up activity. Laughter, practicing gratitude, meditation, and exercise all boost our mood. At the beginning of class, sharing a joke or relating a funny incident can elicit laughter. One colleague has a joke of the day segment. At other times, spontaneous laughter occurs during the course of instruction, especially if teachers who appear infallible make a mistake. Asking students to name three things they are grateful for that day can also help them focus on the positive."

—Bilquis Ahmed, South Bay Adult School

Community Connections

Creating community through shared ideas and common experiences within the classroom also spurred "Aha!" moments. Lessons involving peer collaboration and opportunities to learn together helped many students make curricular connections and view content through a different lens of learning.

We will explore the cultivation of a supportive community and relationship building further in upcoming Retention Anchors. For now, let's note the direct correlation between these factors and priming the adult brain to experience breakthroughs in learning.

"Discussions unfolded, revealing personal challenges, obstacles, and goals. The students were extremely transparent with each other. Several 'Aha!' moments were revealed as they began to further develop connections with their new classmates."

—Faye Ainsworth, Louisiana Delta Community College

"If [students] are invested in the class, feel like they are learning, and see a better future for themselves, they are more likely to put in a little more effort to stay in the class."

—Lyle Ring, Briya Public Charter School

"With trust, students can take risks, express themselves, and allow for mistakes. Adult students are typically, but not always, focused on practical goals, but community building is often something most of them crave. Often, their lives can be isolating, and their adult education class may be one place where they feel comfortable expressing themselves."

—Lyle Ring, Briya Public Charter School

Building Background

PLC educators also discovered that building background knowledge linked to relevant content was extremely effective when applying Just-In-Time Learning. Equipping students with introductory knowledge strengthened connections, facilitated understanding, and allowed for practical application. Teachers found that pre-teaching vocabulary, reviewing steps to a process, and using analogies, metaphors, and relatable anecdotes helped connect students to what they already know, leading to deeper understanding and moments of clarity.

"We must somehow help [students] connect new knowledge to some past experience. New knowledge needs a framework to be incorporated. New knowledge that does not fit can simply be discarded. Before a new lesson, it helps to get students thinking about what they know about a subject so that they can more easily 'file' the new knowledge."

—Tracy Reid, SUNY Morrisville

"I found that by asking my students what helps them learn and using those techniques in class, along with connecting their background knowledge and real-life scenarios to the assignment, it [helped] with comprehension."

—Nikki Andruschak Neal,
Santa Cruz County

Planned Reflection

Additionally, PLC researchers noted the importance of planning time for student reflection. As Harvard researcher Joseph Badaracco (2020) and author of *Step Back: How to Bring the Art of Reflection into Your Busy Life* writes, "Silence and solitude nurture precious eureka moments." By asking open-ended questions that encourage critical thinking, problem-solving, and personal contemplation, teachers can help to stimulate the part of the brain known to engage in creative troubleshooting.

Allowing extra processing time for adult learning, which is slower but deeper, is imperative. Planning time to reflect and process new information is critical. The circular pattern of learning, applying, and reflecting allows students to digest what they've learned. Opportunities for reflection further strengthen connections between prior knowledge and newly introduced concepts.

Repetition

Repetition also emerged as an important, albeit slower, catalyst for clarity. Many PLC members found that the coveted "light-bulb" moment is better characterized as a dimmer switch. Students may instead experience a gradual "Aaaaaaaaaaaaaaaha!" moment rather than a single epiphany.

Just as time for reflection encourages learning, many students must work through content and pertinent examples multiple times to experience that click of understanding. In their lesson

experiments, PLC educators discovered that creating opportunities for repeated practice prompted many learners to build confidence and better apply what they learned. While we all crave instant understanding, in many cases, true comprehension arrives after lengthy exposure.

> *"Discussions should be framed with questions that help provoke deeper thinking and understanding. Students should be allowed time and space for reflection so that the adult learner can process what they are learning before moving on."*
>
> — Christina Smith,
> Goodwill Easter Seals of the Gulf Coast

"We had to practice many more times than just the initial lesson before the student had adequate exposure. I could not get the 'Aha!' moment in one lesson as much as I tried. [The students] needed repeated exposure and review to internalize the content to become fluent with the material."

—Bilquis Ahmed, South Bay Adult School

"Change occurs over time and often creates the right scenario and effect for the adult learner's 'Aha!' experience, which both encourages and urges the learner on but also appears to extend past the end of the course or learning experience."

—Ricardo Bellon, Suncoast Technical College

ACTIVITIES AND APPLICATIONS

Let's recall the **three key attributes** of Just-in-Time Learning (page 25) and consider ways to put these components into practice.

 *Immediate*

Have you ever turned to the internet to solve a problem? Perhaps something in your home is broken, your car is making a strange sound, or you just can't remove that stubborn grass stain! When something goes awry, you need help right away. You search for a solution, read a tutorial, or watch a short video, and address your problem immediately. You don't need advice on routine maintenance or future issues at that moment; you need a rapid resolution. This scenario is a fitting example of how Just-in-Time Learning can be combined with real-time access to information to achieve prompt and practical results. However, producing this immediacy in the adult-ed classroom can be challenging.

Teachers need to be flexible. Discovering the needs and career aspirations of your students is one thing. But articulating applicable examples of transferable skills and tangential information is another. The ability to quickly pivot from planned instruction and capitalize on teachable moments can be intimidating without an arsenal of ideas to utilize. Consider completing the brief **Scoring Activity** (see Appendix D) that can help prepare you for instructional flexibility.

Once you complete the chart, jot a few things down as ideas that emerge about the following question:

How might you better equip yourself with relevant examples for students with unique passions or career paths?

 *Predictive*

In reviewing their JITL lessons, the PLC deemed pre-planning essential in creating "Aha!" moments. It takes time and forethought to set the stage for learning epiphanies. Before structuring a lesson, it is helpful to think through what students already know, how they have approached previous problems, and what they might need to connect to the content. Choose a core lesson in a specific content area (e.g., Adding Fractions in Mathematics or Main Idea in Reading) and then try working through the questions below.

What questions do students have about this subject? How can you prepare to answer those queries?

What additional content relates to this lesson? What connections have previous students mentioned?

How can you prepare to connect relatable examples to the core topic?

 *Targeted*

Today's teachers have access to more data than ever before. Formal and informal assessments, observations, student surveys, measurable skills reports, and countless other tools exist to illuminate individual student needs. Examining these needs at a granular level helps students identify their next step toward growth. Once these elements are revealed, students can set specific goals, and educators can create targeted instruction. Consider the following questions and complete the chart below. *What tools do you currently use to identify learning gaps? How do you use those tools to design targeted instruction? How can you better leverage these assessments to tailor classroom lessons and activities?*

Tool	What does it show?	How can I use this information to address students' needs?
Essential Education's Student Progress Report	*Identifies specific skill gaps.*	• *Review exercises to address basics* • *Repeated practice of required skill*

TOP TAKEAWAYS

Capitalizing on the Now: Applying Just-In-Time Learning

- *Just-In-Time Learning strategies set the stage for "Aha!" moments.* When instruction is intentional and personally applicable, students are better able to understand a concept or develop a skill.

- *There are three characteristics of Just-In-Time Learning instruction:*

  1. Immediate– Instruction that engages students in the moment.
  2. Predictive– Instruction that anticipates what is needed and when it will be needed.
  3. Targeted– Instruction that aims to address a distinct learning gap.

- *Collective research highlights six effective elements of Just-In-Time Learning:*

  1. Mood and excitement– A positive classroom environment is foundational for student growth.
  2. Shared ideas– Creating community through common experiences spurs "Aha!" moments.
  3. Background knowledge– Links to relevant content fuel Just-In-Time Learning strategies.
  4. Speed of instruction– Allowing extra processing time for adult learning is imperative.
  5. Student reflection– Planning time to reflect and process new information is critical.
  6. Repetition– Revisiting important concepts is a catalyst for clarity.

ANCHOR CONNECTION

The connection between Retention Anchor 1 and Anchor 2 is clear. With a robust understanding of adult student demographics, we can better design instruction that meets practical needs and forms a foundation for student success. Learning is most effective when students' needs and goals are recognized and supported.

Let's look ahead. How might these two Retention Anchors connect to Anchors yet to be explored? How will these pieces collectively support student retention?

Use the following questions to note potential connections between retention supporting factors.

How can knowing your students and applying JITL strategies impact your ability to create timely and relevant instruction?

How can knowing your students and using JITL strategies foster an environment for student success?

How can understanding your students and applying JITL strategies help to enhance student and class relationships?

How can knowing your students and using JITL strategies aid in measuring student progress?

How can knowing your students and applying JITL strategies facilitate professional development?

Quick Reflection

Continue to reflect as we investigate further Retention Anchors and think deeply about the connections between each topic. The goal is to create a balanced "retention ship" capable of maintaining and growing student attendance and continuance.

SUPPORT FROM ESSENTIAL EDUCATION

Students and educators succeed when timely, relevant content is easy to access and manage. Essential Education's products provide on-demand lessons expertly designed to meet the Just-in-Time learning needs of busy adults. Our adaptive instruction model provides students with support and guidance to address identified skill gaps. A user-friendly LMS provides detailed reports, allowing teachers to pinpoint students' strengths and struggles and guide learners in their next steps.

Skill mastery is faster and more efficient because students can focus on what they need, when they need it. Opportunities for reflection and review support the repetition many adults need to build problem-solving skills and long-term memory. Just-in-Time Learning is also supported by:

Customized pre-assessments to focus on the exact skills needed. Individualized student assessments create a foundation for personal success. Skills-aligned reports enable educators to target immediate needs and improve measurable skill gains over time.

Short online video instruction to provide flexibility for busy students. Essential Education lessons are available 24 hours a day, seven days a week. Content is accessible to students at their exact moment of need. Instruction is brief, but comprehensive, allowing for targeted, time-conscious skill development.

Print resources and workbooks to support blended learning. Supplemental written materials are available to students needing extra instruction and practice. All workbook content is aligned to online lessons, creating a robust and multi-faceted learning experience.

Mobile-friendly lessons to meet students on the go. Just-In-Time Learning requires on-demand access. Essential Education content is intentionally designed to meet the needs of busy working adults. Lessons are portable and can be completed on hundreds of mobile devices, allowing students to make the most of their study time outside of class.

Quizzes and practice tests to allow for self-evaluation. Students can measure their personal progress through skills-based assessments. They receive immediate feedback and additional instruction through answer explanations and review activities.

Contextualized content to provide real-world connections. All Essential Education courses are built for adult learners. Relatable characters, real-world examples, and workplace connections help students link academic concepts to their daily lives, deepening long-term understanding and engagement.

RETENTION ANCHOR 3/

CREATING CULTURE

FOSTERING AN ENVIRONMENT FOR STUDENT SUCCESS

SETTING THE STAGE

You are likely starting to get the pattern here—we started with the "who" in order to help educators better understand their students and communities. We examined the "what" and discussed how to tailor instruction to help our students become people capable of taking their next step. Now we come to the "where." Where does effective learning take place? What are the markers of a culture and a learning environment that support adult student success? Does classroom culture naturally occur, or is it influenced and nurtured by its teachers and students?

Much can be said about how "culture" impacts performance and student retention rates. Before we jump into the research and explore this topic, you'll need to lay some groundwork. Spend some time reflecting on the following questions.

What does the term "culture" mean to you? Consider this as it relates to the learning environment you create as an educator.

Think through some examples of culture you have seen or been a part of. Sports teams, clubs, jobs, volunteer organizations, and other interest groups form distinct cultural norms. What was positive? What was negative? How much "just happened," and how much was intentional? Who drove the culture?

Retention Anchor 3: Creating Culture

What elements of your program or class culture are deeply embedded? What factors seem fluid?

What barriers hinder changing or improving the culture around you? Self-reflection is powerful and can profoundly impact your ability to shape a learning environment.

REVIEWING THE RESEARCH

Culture, by definition, can also mean to cultivate or grow. When scientists send something to be cultured, they ask lab technicians to expose various organic materials to catalytic conditions to see what "grows." Classroom culture can be described similarly. A group of individuals with common characteristics, yet vastly different needs, receive learning opportunities in an environment that attempts to yield growth (or the ability to take next steps). As an educator, you create the classroom environment that acts as the catalyst.

Each of us has multiple "cultures" in our lives. Workplaces, families, circles of friends, and extracurricular hobbies have specific cultural traits. Whether intentionally planned or shaped by happenstance, a group dynamic is quite powerful. Our thoughts, attitudes, beliefs, and even our physical appearance and mannerisms can be significantly shaped by the cultures we are immersed in. Entrepreneur and motivational speaker Jim Rohn defined it this way: "We are the average of the five people we spend the most time with." Everyone brings something unique to the group, but research has repeatedly shown that we are more influenced by our environment than we may think. The cultures in which we interact have many benefits and consequences stemming from the group's defined (and often undefined) social norms. In other words, who and what we surround ourselves with matters.

"Learning doesn't happen in a vacuum. Your classroom community is made up of individuals with diverse identities, backgrounds, and experiences; the act of learning is intertwined with a variety of socioemotional influences."

—The Ohio State University

Do a quick internet search on successful culture. You will be flooded with research, opinions, anecdotes, success stories, and multiple lists of best practices. From nonprofits and corporations to sports and education, various genres of culture creators provide exceptional insight into what best supports an ideal group dynamic. While there are nuances to each, and the buzzwords change from time to time, there is a great deal of agreement as to what characteristics create an effective culture in any setting.

We've narrowed it down to this: growth environments are **defined**, **reflective**, and **intentional**.

 *Defined*

Teachers and administrators must purposefully define the culture they want to create. Reviewing the program's mission, vision, and values is a terrific place to begin. Routine internal development that prompts and encourages all staff to embrace shared objectives significantly contributes to educator and student morale. As you define a culture that fosters student success and continuance at a more minute level, ask yourself, What are the non-negotiables? What are the adjectives you would use to describe your desired classroom or program culture?

Quick Reflection

Imagine you are dining in a restaurant. At an adjacent booth, you hear a group of people discussing your program or classroom. What are the things you would hope to hear? What are the things you would never want to hear? These hypothetical responses will show the attributes you most want to create or avoid while giving you a starting point to analyze where you are. They are tough questions because the responses could be difficult to digest. However, constructive criticism is invaluable in cultivating a healthy, authentic environment. Note your thoughts below.

Here are a few descriptive terms to get you started. Circle or highlight the **culture characteristics** that stand out to you, or add your own.

Collaborative	Motivating	Inclusive	Encouraging
Empathetic	Comfortable	Productive	Flexible
Innovative	Autonomous	Engaging	Purposeful

With your desired characteristics in mind, you can better define the environment in which your students will thrive. Most queries about culture inevitably lead to a discussion about perception and reality. The hard truth is that our perceptions of our program and classroom environments may differ significantly from those of our students. Because personal perception shapes reality, obtaining a clear, honest picture of current culture is vital to building and sustaining future growth.

Quick Reflection

How close are you? Revisit the list of **culture characteristics** (page 47) you chose above and rate them from 1 to 10, with 10 meaning you have no doubt that the characteristic of your environment is strong and 1 indicating that you have a lot of work to do.

Want to take it a step further? Which characteristics are "data-based" (can be measured) versus "perception-based" (open to personal interpretation)? Be sure to make some notes for reference.

> *"As an educator, I must realize that my students will view the classroom culture differently than I do. I also must realize that they will each view it differently from each other."*
>
> —Nikki Andruschak Neal, Santa Cruz Continuing Education

 *Reflective*

The reflective component of culture should exist at every stage of development. Educators must first consider what ideal culture looks like and articulate the specific characteristics they want to exemplify. Reflection must also include opportunities for routine staff and student feedback to establish a baseline and measure the effectiveness of responsive strategies. The information obtained in ongoing evaluation aids teachers and administrators in creating targeted initiatives to shore up the strengths of the current culture and formulate an action plan to address areas of need.

When all group members of a community feel heard and understood, engagement increases as a sense of belonging is established. Anonymous surveys, "exit" tickets, peer observations, and full program collaboration opportunities are terrific ways to explore the complexities of a learning culture. Embracing and responding to quality feedback is not only essential for program improvement, but it is also an excellent trait to model for students hoping to better themselves and their lives. When educators openly emulate growth characteristics, students have a front-row seat to personal and professional development. The spirit of life-long learning is contagious, sparks motivation, and inspires determination.

 Intentional

With defined goals and solid feedback in hand, educators can form an intentional plan to support student success through culture. When designing

Quick Reflection

How well do you process feedback? Do you have approaches in place to measure student/teacher perspectives? If yes, how do you use that information? If not, what's holding you back?

an approach unique to the group's needs, carefully consider how to best communicate goals for improvement, and think through targeted activities to achieve those goals. Clear program objectives and specific initiatives set well-defined expectations and establish accountability for all learning community members.

Collaboration at this stage of culture development is essential, as all perspectives (or realities) must be considered. This is especially important in adult education classrooms because adult students thrive when given greater control and autonomy in learning. This independence includes building the environment in which learning takes place. As you walk through these reflection exercises, consider individual classroom culture and the overall program environment. Collective culture is most effective when there are shared organizational values.

Authentic discussions with staff and students will help clarify the next steps in culture development and reinforce the program's vision. This type of "buy-in" from all community members is crucial to creating an environment that promotes success. Strong cultures flourish when everyone runs in the same direction with eyes fixed on a common goal. This boosts mood and excitement (priming the brain for "Aha!" moments), and a sense of belonging prompts acceptance and continued participation. Relationships foster community and create something special that everyone wants to be a part of. In this respect, an academic culture of partnership facilitates solid student retention and can significantly improve educator motivation and commitment.

Quick Reflection

Do you have any immediate thoughts for designing, reflecting on, and implementing positive culture shifts? Take some notes here to revisit later.

"A positive school climate can improve students' academic achievement, attendance, engagement, and behavior, as well as teacher satisfaction and retention."

—Arianna Prothero, Education Week

EVALUATION AND REFLECTION

"Sounds good. Sign me up!" We now have a clearer idea of why culture is important and some common qualities of best practices, but how does all of this play out in real adult education classrooms?

We posed this question to the PLC and tasked the members with completing an **Independent Culture Workshop** (see Appendix E). Utilizing evaluation tools provided by Essential Education, members were asked to define and evaluate ideal and current classroom or program cultures. Instructions prompted participants to include both educator and student reflections. Each participant chose one area of improvement, planned to address that area intentionally, and shared their findings and strategies with the group. The results were equal parts illuminating and inspiring.

The descriptive adjectives were abundant when analyzing the "non-negotiables" of ideal classroom culture. While the assignment asked PLC members to indicate three key descriptors, many expressed that listing only three terms was restrictive. The educators surveyed want their classroom environments to be known for numerous positive qualities! Despite their initial skepticism, the PLC members worked to narrow their priorities to three top characteristics.

The ideal adult education program should be **safe and comfortable**, **meaningful**, and **growth-oriented**.

> *"A classroom climate that is safe and conducive to learning, with positive rapport among all participants, is essential for adult learners."*
>
> —Dr. Wendy Kline, Literacy Kansas City

Safe and Comfortable

Learning is wrought with emotion. Excitement in gaining new knowledge, fear of failure, embarrassment after mistakes, and triumph in success make academia a non-scientific, feelings-driven process. Cultivating classroom positivity motivates students to excel, while negative emotions can significantly hinder learning. Predictably, educators denote creating a safe and comfortable learning environment is utmost importance.

PLC contributor Kelly Grudowski defined a safe school culture as one that "allows students to feel confident and comfortable when making mistakes. When students feel safe, they take more chances in their learning." The risk required to develop a new skill is intimidating to any learner. Those risks can seem even more daunting for students with less than favorable experiences in previous school environments. To this end, teachers must not only address the support factors of their current classroom culture but combat the ghosts of learning past that may still be haunting their students.

Susan Spradlin of Tennessee College of Applied Technology echoed this reflection by sharing, "Without first feeling safe, students will not have the open-mindedness needed to grow. Without empathy, students could feel isolated, misunderstood, or judged. All of which deter the motivation to learn." To support their findings, several PLC educators referenced a recent report from The Ohio State University, where researchers discovered significant ties between student learning and a supportive community.

The article, titled "Shaping a Positive Learning Environment," noted, "When you create an environment where students feel accepted, seen, and valued, they are more likely to persist" (The Ohio State University, n.d.).

Clearly, classroom safety and comfort have direct links to student engagement and retention. But perhaps students aren't the only ones who need a sense of security to excel in the classroom. Bilquis Ahmed shared that the culture at South Bay Adult School in Redondo Beach, California, promotes safety in learning from a top-down perspective. "Our classrooms are safe places where students [and teachers] can make mistakes. Mistakes are seen as opportunities for learning. Teachers openly admit when they make mistakes while modeling how to correct them. When teachers do not know something, they openly admit it. Some will consult Google for clarification in front of the students; others will bring a neighboring teacher into the class to answer the question." Teachers feel free to take a collective breath, glean support from their colleagues, and grow professionally without fearing reprimand or distrust in their craft.

Administrator Tracy Reid noted a similar conclusion, using exemplary corporate culture as a guide for building educational environments. Similarly, with a commitment to program goals and a safety net of support, educators feel empowered and comfortable taking the risks they need to try new instructional strategies. To this end, student retention and teacher retention are tightly aligned.

"When employees feel that the company values and supports them, they are more likely to remain with the company long-term. This helps create a sense of loyalty and belonging among the employees and ultimately contributes to the business's success."

—Tracy Reid, SUNY Morrisville

"Schools should be safe places where students and staff develop strong relationships, feel empowered, and have a sense of belonging."

—Laura Encalade, National Institute for Excellence in Teaching

An intentional effort to model and promote emotional safety and comfort in the classroom is the heart of Social and Emotional Learning, or SEL. This developmental process has been proven repeatedly to have a profound ripple effect in improving outcomes for all members of a learning community. For some educators, this aspect of teaching may not have "made it into the brochure," but it is nonetheless a powerful and necessary component of effective instruction.

Humans need connection to thrive. Those connections simply cannot be sustained without a foundation of rapport and trust. We will discuss the relationship connection to retention in the next Anchor. For now, we cannot overlook the value of creating safe spaces in building a culture that supports student (and educator) success.

"Implementing these principles requires the adult educator to be technically proficient in content and program planning areas as well as highly competent in interpersonal and human relation skills."

—Michael W. Galbraith,
Adult Learning Methods: A Guide for Effective Instruction

Meaningful

Creating a meaningful environment was also top of mind as PLC educators reflected on ideal classroom culture. Stop for a moment and consider this term.

Adult educator and PLC member Kelly Grudowski defines a meaningful educational environment as "learning [that] connects lessons with students' needs [and] creates coursework that benefits students' lives." From the demographic research we explored regarding adult learners' common characteristics and needs, we know this connection is highly important. Adult students need to see direct links between their learning and their daily lives and goals.

Quick Reflection

What does creating a meaningful learning environment mean to you?

"Content that draws from real-world examples and relatable scenarios and builds on direct experience will lead to a more meaningful understanding of the subject. Both the immediate, short-term relevancy and the long-term benefits of engaging with the content should be highlighted in such a way that the learner will immediately dedicate themselves to learning."

—Ivan Andreev, Valamis

Not only do we have observational and experiential evidence that adults need highly contextualized learning, this truth is also firmly supported by neuroscientific research. While studies indicate that adults learn more slowly than children, those same studies reveal the rich resources (past experiences, prior knowledge, and personal motivation) that can be tapped for adult learning to have more profound long-term results.

The landscape of the adult education classroom is diverse, and the differentiation needed to engage and provide applicable meaning for all learners is not without its challenges. Grudowski notes, "Meaningful learning is one of the most important characteristics to adult students but is also one of the hardest to implement. The idea of making every lesson meaningful sounds great, but it is not always possible to turn the required curriculum into something relevant to adult life."

This is where adult educators must push themselves to be strategically creative when planning instruction for adult learners. In targeting this need within her program, Grudowski notes the value of laying a foundation for real-world connections before students enter the classroom. She writes, "We need to find out their goals, and if they don't [have goals], we [need] to teach them the steps to set obtainable goals. It will also be imperative to find out what interests each student in order to help them select elective courses or use their interests as motivation. Once we get the students on their educational path, we need to present them with the benefits of learning the material in the coursework. This approach can motivate our adult learners if they know how it will impact their futures."

"The adult brain is different from the child's. It's like comparing an untouched canvas to an almost-finished painting. Each stroke, each color, and each layer represents different life experiences, learned skills, and absorbed knowledge. This complexity shapes the way adults learn, and these differences are what adult learning theories aim to address."

—Tibi Puiu, ZME Science

What if there is no apparent connection between required content and student interests or career-based skills? Can learning still be meaningful? Absolutely! The link for meaning lies in constantly reinforcing the value of problem-solving. Critical thinking and reasoning skills apply to nearly all personal and work-based interactions. Adult learning programs providing high school equivalency prep, job readiness, and basic skills education are teeming with opportunities to link acquired knowledge to countless real-world scenarios.

*"Problem-solving
is the need of the
hour! When students
practice problem-solving
consistently, they can
develop better social and
situational awareness. They
will also learn to manage time
properly and develop patience."*

—HCL Jigsaw,
"21st Century Skills: Why is Problem-solving the Need of the Hour for School Students?"

Quick Reflection

Do you or your program have systems or processes to learn the interests and goals of your students? How could you acquire that valuable information to create a meaningful learning environment?

Quick Reflection

Are you intentionally teaching or drawing attention to problem-solving? What small changes could you make to target these meaningful skills?

Consider this list of tips from the University of Waterloo's Center for Teaching Excellence (n.d.) curated to build a culture of adult learning linked to meaningful problem-solving skills.

- **Model problem-solving methods through "think-alouds."** Walk your students through test questions, math problems, writing assignments, reading approaches, or similar assignments, and indicate your personal thought process along the way. Encourage them to do the same to develop corresponding strategies.

- **Note problem-solving skills in context.** Use real-life problems in explanations, examples, and exams. Teach problem-solving as a specific, multi-use skill.

- **Help students understand the problem.** Finding the answer to "How?" will be easier if students can answer the questions "What?" and "Why?"

- **Take time.** Allow time for understanding the problem and defining the goal when planning instruction. This includes specific allotments for answering questions and noting and correcting mistakes.

- **Solicit suggestions.** Ask students to predict "what would happen if ..." or explain why something happened. This is an essential factor in developing analytical and deductive thinking skills. Encourage students to evaluate their "go-to" problem-solving strategies.

- **Link mistakes to learning.** To err is human. Drawing attention to the application of what is learned is powerful.

Growth-Oriented

After discussing the significance of an adult learning environment that promotes meaningful interactions in a safe environment, PLC researchers collectively turned to the importance of building a growth-oriented culture. As collaborative discussions around growth in the adult education classroom began to unfold, a more extensive dialogue arose surrounding one pivotal term: mindset.

World-renowned human motivation and success researcher Carol Dweck describes mindset as falling into two distinct categories—fixed and growth ("Carol Dweck: A Summary of the Two Mindsets," n.d.). Within a fixed mindset, intelligence is static. Individuals with this mindset avoid obstacles, lack perseverance, and see little to no value in their efforts. They tend to ignore feedback and often feel threatened or discouraged by the success of others. However, those with a growth mindset view intelligence as something that can be developed. They learn to embrace challenges, persist amid setbacks, see effort as achievement, understand the importance of constructive criticism, and gain inspiration and motivation from the success of others.

Many adult students must fight to maintain a positive mindset. Negative, often painful past educational experiences are a formidable foe in the adult classroom. Hardworking adult students face many challenges outside the classroom that teachers and administrators have little power to change. They often feel overwhelmed and doubt their ability to succeed within their current circumstances. The feeling of failure is palpable in many adult learning programs.

Dweck recognizes the potential paralysis of this type of pain but offers an alternative. In her book Mindset: The New Psychology of Success, she states, "In the growth mindset, failure can be a painful experience. But it doesn't define you. It's a problem to be faced, dealt with, and learned from" ("Carol Dweck: A Summary of the Two Mindsets," n.d.). However, this may seem easier said than done because living out that principle requires a massive evolution in thought and a dramatic shift in mindset.

Or does it? Could the enormity of hurtful, self-doubt-yielding experiences be upturned with the application of one 3-letter word: yet? Dweck's findings say yes. In her powerful TED Talk, "The Power of Believing You Can Improve," Dweck shares the following story:

> ### TED Talk:
> ### "The Power of Believing You Can Improve"
>
> *I heard about a high school in Chicago where students had to pass a certain number of courses to graduate, and if they didn't pass a course, they got the grade "Not Yet." And I thought that was fantastic because if you get a failing grade, you think, I'm nothing. I'm nowhere. But if you get the grade "Not Yet," you understand that you're on a learning curve. It gives you a path into the future.*
>
> *"Not Yet" also gave me insight into a critical event early in my career, a real turning point. I wanted to see how children coped with challenge and difficulty, so*

"*Of the many challenges educators face, one of the most formidable—and least obvious—is student mindset. Teaching students to comprehend, absorb, and apply new material and concepts is challenging under any circumstances. The undertaking is much greater, however, when students doubt their ability to learn.*"

— American University School of Education

I gave 10-year-olds problems that were slightly too hard for them. Some of them reacted in a shockingly positive way. They said things like, "I love a challenge," or, "You know, I was hoping this would be informative." They understood that their abilities could be developed. They had what I call a growth mindset. But other students felt it was tragic, catastrophic. From their more fixed mindset perspective, their intelligence had been up for judgment, and they failed. Instead of luxuriating in the power of yet, they were gripped in the tyranny of now.

So what do they do next? I'll tell you what they do next. In one study, they told us they would probably cheat the next time instead of studying more if they failed a test. In another study, after a failure, they looked for someone who did worse than they did so they could feel really good about themselves. And in study after study, they have run from difficulty. Scientists measured the electrical activity from the brain as students confronted an error. On the left, you see the fixed mindset students. There's hardly any activity. They run from the error. They don't engage with it. But on the right, you have the students with the growth mindset, the idea that abilities can be developed. They engage deeply. Their brain is on fire with yet. They engage deeply. They process the error. They learn from it, and they correct it. ("Carol Dweck: A Summary of the Two Mindsets," n.d.).

If the human brain processes challenges this way in childhood, it's no wonder developing a growth mindset can be a tremendous hurdle for adult learners. In short, while educators can draw on the extended experiences of adults to create engaging instruction, they are simultaneously combatting a lifetime of mistakes and failures. We noted this obstacle in creating a classroom environment of safety and revisited it here as a deterrent to growth. Are adult learners doomed to continuously be plagued by the past, or is there a way to use their advanced life experiences to their advantage?

While exploring this crucial topic, PLC educator Lyle Ring of Briya Public Charter School (Washington, D.C.) leaned into Jack Mezirow's Transformative Learning Theory (TLT) principles. Mezirow theorized that adult students have learning opportunities connected to their past experiences. Our PLC members have observed this connection firsthand. As we discussed in the first Anchor, the link between coursework and real-world experiences is a vehicle for cultivating meaningful learning. But Mezirow's work took that truth further, emphasizing that an adult learner's critical reflection and review of their experiences could transform their understanding. Because children do not have the breadth of life experiences from which to draw, they often lack the ability to undergo a similar degree of transformation. In essence, TLT suggests that adult learners uniquely possess the ability to make the mindset leaps required for growth because they have a library of experiences (both negative and positive) from which to draw. It's all in how those experiences are harnessed and shaped.

"Mezirow found that adult learning involves taking the very things we believed and thought as a child and letting critical reflection and teaching impact the transformation to what we should believe and understand now. Mezirow's theory has developed into a larger idea that our worldview is changed the more we learn, and that helps us grasp new concepts and ideas."

— Western Governors University

If Mezirow's theory holds, the opportunity and responsibility within the adult education classroom reach immeasurable strength. If we are to truly impact the lives of our students and cultivate a culture of perseverance, we must passionately tackle mindset head-on. Caring professionals can shape a learning environment that provides studen`ts the tools to improve their education, develop skills, overcome self-doubt, and build the resilience to push through challenges. There is tremendous opportunity and responsibility in creating a culture that fosters life change. We must develop strategies to enable adults to see purpose in the painful experiences of their past and equip them with the tools needed to accomplish their goals.

As Ring evaluated the role of a growth mindset in effective classroom culture, he highlighted the need to convince students of the value of progress over performance. As discussed in the previous Retention Anchors, we know this element is of primary importance to adult learners because they thrive in seeing the results of their efforts. While many get stuck on unmet performance goals, a growth mindset rests on celebrating effort-based objectives and outcomes over time.

As Ring pondered these principles with his colleagues, he offered a few collective strategies to create a growth-oriented culture in the adult education classroom.

1. Schedule routine conferences to check in with students and share areas of improvement and those needing further development.

2. Provide students with tools to view progress over time. Point out and celebrate milestones and gains.

3. Concentrate on the process of producing work rather than solely assessing the results.

4. Allow opportunities for class and individual reflections on learning and teaching. Acknowledge and respond to suggestions in instruction.

5. Explicitly teach a growth mindset, how the human mind develops, and how learning happens.

Note the collaborative nature of Ring's suggestions. Harnessing the adult learner's desire for autonomy, these techniques allow students to exercise more control in their learning. They see that learning isn't something that happens to them. It's a process in which they are the main characters, writing their own success story. Our lives are not linear. Success doesn't rest in the flip of a switch. It develops over time, with many ups and downs. Progress is cultivated by lessons learned, experiences shared, and environments that encourage growth.

With the vision of an ideal student success culture top of mind, PLC members dove into the most challenging culture work of all: sorting

Quick Reflection

Add to the strategies suggested above. What mindset-building activities come to mind?

perception from reality. Using survey tools provided within the **Independent Culture Workshop** (see Appendix E), students and staff used this opportunity to express their thoughts on classroom and program culture.

There were celebrated "wins," as educators discovered that many of their positive perceptions were shared by their students and other learning community members. Many took encouragement in seeing some of their "non-negotiables" were, in fact, substantial components of their classroom or program environment. The harder pill to swallow came in discovering areas where perception didn't quite meet reality.

As PLC members shared areas of cultural concern, once again, common threads emerged. While each educator identified needs specific to their unique population, nearly all groups surveyed discovered these three areas needed improvement: greater student-to-student collaboration, a deeper understanding of student needs, and increased use of evaluation-based practices.

Student-to-Student Collaboration

What connections come to mind when you hear the word collaboration in an academic setting? Teacher-to-student collaboration? Student-to-student collaboration? Teacher-to-teacher collaboration? Teacher-to-admin collaboration? Yes, yes, and yes! Collaboration within a learning community includes each of these elements. However, as PLC members isolated variables within this area of concern, they discovered that increased opportunities for student-to-student collaboration were the top need.

"There is definitely room for improvement related to classroom safety. I want students to feel comfortable collaborating together."

—Cherie Goranites, Bonny Eagle Adult Education

"Much can be done in the classroom to encourage student participation and support. Many students will look to their fellow students for support and information as they face challenges."

—Lyle Ring, Briya Public Charter School

"One area [that] could improve is collaboration. It is more and more evident that we do not know how to get along with others or understand it's okay to 'agree to disagree.' Collaboration can also springboard empathy and meaning."

— Susan Spradlin,
Tennessee College of Applied Technology

"If an adult does not feel they are a part of the group, it will impact their learning, and therefore, it will impact their desire to stay in the class. Encouraging group participation, even in small groups, will bring together the students. Whether in a physical classroom or a virtual online session, forming and maintaining relationships between classmates will improve student retention."

— Nikki Andruschak Neal, Santa Cruz Continuing Education

In exploring the expressed desire for greater collaboration among students, PLC educator Cherie Goranites of Bonny Eagle Adult Education in Maine referenced the article "What Are Norms and Why Do They Matter?" from the California Academy of Sciences (n.d.).

> "Trust among participants [makes] sure that everyone feels that they will be heard, that attention is paid to inclusive behavior, and that there is space and time for questions and contributions from all participants."

—Cherie Goranites, Bonny Eagle Adult Education

Goranites explained that she uncovered a distinct link between student-student collaboration and culture-defining feelings of safety and comfort within her classroom. She writes, "I realized that my expectations regarding classroom interactions could be more clearly defined. This was confirmed by the responses to [survey] questions related to collaboration, i.e., asking peers questions and feeling comfortable discussing their work with their classmates. Students only 'kind of' agreed with these statements. Although I provide directions for group work, I know that I don't have agreed-upon group norms in my classroom. A clear set of group norms could greatly improve students' comfort levels and feelings of safety, providing them with a better sense of belonging."

Susan Spradlin of Tennessee College of Applied Technology reached similar conclusions in her PLC research, as she also noted the correlation between student-student collaboration and creating a safe learning environment. She shares, "For collaboration to be effective, students must first feel safe to share and realize others in the class have similar situations for problems they face."

After pondering specific ways to improve peer collaboration in her classroom, Spradlin outlined these future activities she hopes to set in motion. "To foster safety and sharing, I would begin by introducing a getting-to-know-each-other time at the beginning of each class period. This could be done over breakfast or anything that would create a relaxed atmosphere. If students are struggling to talk to one another, I would provide some conversation starters, sentence stems, or something to open the floor for relaxing and chatting. Next, I would strategically pair students together to solve a problem or complete a simple project. By working just with one other person, confidence can begin to shine, and both would feel important to the team. I would continue adding students to create a larger team effort in completing or analyzing the task at hand. I could see this ending with a group project where each group contributes a part of the whole, bigger outcome."

Spradlin also suggested a specific activity for high school equivalency educators hoping to improve student collaboration: "Have a group of students create a guide to the HiSET [GED] experience. Each group could take a particular topic or subject and create a section for the guide to leave for the next group. [They] would decide what information to include, what details to offer, and any tips they experienced during their time in adult education. After each group has developed their section, the class as a whole could make the end guide together. The students would develop their writing and math skills as they create [the] layout."

Both Goranites and Spradlin believe that peer collaboration has direct ties to student retention. Collaboration efforts seek to reduce isolation and anxiety, create a sense of accountability, and link students to something larger than themselves. Spradlin states, "If [students] come to class knowing that they are not alone, it could create motivation to attend, help others, and know the group depends on [them]."

Larger studies on collaborative learning cite positive peer interaction as a powerful element of student growth and progress. Cornell University Center for Teaching Innovation researchers (n.d.) found that "educational experiences that are

Quick Reflection

Do you intentionally plan activities to encourage student-student collaboration? Which of Cornell's examples could you integrate to enhance this element of your classroom/program culture?

active, social, contextual, engaging, and student-owned lead to deeper learning." The university's teaching resources outlined these additional benefits of student collaboration in the classroom:

- Development of higher-level thinking, oral communication, self-management, and leadership skills.

- Exposure to and an increase in understanding of diverse perspectives.

- Preparation for real-life social and employment situations.

- Increase in student retention, self-esteem, and responsibility.

The teaching resources also offered a robust list of suggestions to create and maintain a solid collaborative learning community.

- Introduce group work early to set clear student expectations.

- Plan, establish, and clearly communicate ground rules for participation and contributions.

- Provide opportunities for students to develop rapport and group cohesion through icebreakers, team-building, and reflection exercises.

- Develop student reflection skills with self-assessment and peer-assessment activities.

- Debrief. Call on a few students to share a summary of their conclusions. Address any misconceptions or clarify any confusing points. Open the floor for questions.

- Give students time to create a group work plan for deadlines and divide their responsibilities.

- Use group planning examples to model the importance of setting small measurable goals.

Deeper Understanding of Student Needs

The PLC discovered that developing a deeper understanding of student needs is another element of effective culture that requires improvement. Several educators were surprised to learn that some students felt that their teachers and program leaders did not completely understand the complexities of their lives outside the classroom.

Christina Smith, Goodwill Easter Seals of the Gulf Coast (AL), shared her experiences on this topic: "One thing that did surprise me was that some circled 'kind of' on 'my teacher knows my life demands outside of class.' My students come from all walks of life. They are in different places in their lives and education. Some students demand

"The more we know about adult learners, the barriers they face, and how these barriers interfere with their learning, the better we can structure classroom experiences that engage all learners and stimulate both personal growth and reflection."

—Marina Falasca, Universidad Tecnológica Nacional

more attention than others. Some students have hectic schedules and make it to class when they can. I try to keep up with who is out or who is coming to class, but I have a revolving door and many students to keep track of." Chaw Kalayar of Prince George's Community College echoed this concern. She noted her observations confirmed that "listening to students' learning needs, accommodating them, and following up" were cited as areas of concern in student survey results. Because we know that grasping the "who" of adult education is vital, revealing this particular fragile area and devising a support plan is crucial.

Both Smith and Kalayar are now intentionally attempting to respond to feedback regarding student needs. Smith writes, "I am going to start making calls and sending texts and emails to students that miss class three times. I will make these calls and messages on Fridays when I am in my office. We have intake twice a month, so the Fridays that there is no intake, I will dedicate my office time to making the calls, texts, and emails. Hopefully, implementing this will not only improve my communication with my students but increase attendance. When they miss class, I miss them. I will do better in letting them know they are missed and I am here when and if they need me."

To add fuller context to the conversation and a unique perspective, PLC educator LaDonna Torrey with the Kansas Department of Corrections shared this deeply personal reflection.

PLC Conversation:
LaDonna Torrey Personal Reflection

I work in corrections, a challenge from the start. The age difference, race, mentality, and diversity are wide-ranged. It's a daily struggle for many of my students to stay motivated and not give up, as they are not typical adult learners. Due to the restrictions and limitations I am working with, I believe I've put these cultural areas at the back of my to-do list. The areas that need improvement in my classroom are recognizing the demands of students outside of the classroom, their personal goals, and recognition of achievements.

Since my students are incarcerated, I have assumed they don't have anything else in life going on. I need to stop and realize that life doesn't stop for their families on the outside and how it would feel to be unable to help those you love. When students enter my classroom, I try not to look at their prior offenses. Because of this reason, I have not considered thinking about their personal goals right now. I try not to get too close to my students, not realizing that goal setting isn't getting too personal with them. It's them getting in touch with themselves and their journey.

Retention Anchor 3: Creating Culture

The palpable truth within Torrey's words lends special insight for adult educators. Uncovering a student's life goals is a gateway to a better understanding of who the learner is and what motivates them to succeed. Inquiring about a student's personal and professional goals opens the door for educators to make stronger connections. This shows students that their instructors care about them in and out of the classroom. Opportunities to gather that valuable information must be intentional, and follow-up is required for full impact.

PLC educator Ester Garcia is directing her attention to this area of improvement in her current initiatives at Cory Learning Center. To create and maintain a culture that supports student success, Garcia outlined a series of steps for the educators within her program to get a tighter grip on student needs and goals. Using "15+ Strategies to Help With Student Accountability" by Morgan Atkins (2022) as a guide, Garcia focused on the following:

- Prioritize personal relationships by meeting with students individually.

- Create clear expectations. Set specific dates or a cadence of check-ins (weekly, monthly, etc.) to update students on their progress and discuss concerns.

- Be clear with goals and deadlines. Exercise flexible compassion by taking life demands into consideration while emphasizing accountability.

- Keep students engaged throughout the learning process. Create personalized pathways.

- Motivate students by celebrating success.

Quick Reflection

Which of Garcia's initiatives stands out to you? Which are you doing/not doing? Is there one objective you could focus on immediately? What would that entail? How might that intentionally shift the culture of your learning environment?

Evaluation-Based Practices

Getting to the heart of student needs is just one of the many benefits of implementing opportunities for feedback within a learning community. Already noted as a primary element of effective culture and a requirement for a growth mindset, reflection is an invaluable tool. However, many PLC educators found their use of evaluation-based practices in need of improvement. This particular need garners attention, not only due to the many insights gleaned from the **Independent Culture Workshop** (see Appendix E) but also the unexpected value of working through the assignment itself.

Participating educators noted that they "never really used student surveys" or 'hadn't conducted many evaluations." Several noted that while questions about students' goals, interests, and academic backgrounds were asked upon intake or orientation, they were not monitored or updated as the students progressed. In working through this exercise, PLC teachers and administrators were reminded of the importance of routinely assessing all aspects of the student experience and using those insights to create feedback-driven plans for improvement.

In recognizing the need for improved evaluation practices in her adult education program, PLC administrator Sarah Finan of Orion Education and Training committed to filling the feedback gap with opportunities for individual assessment and collaborative group feedback. Using "day one" questionnaires for students and staff and establishing a system of routine follow-up, she will implement a "team huddle" approach. These initiatives will allow all learning community members to take part in addressing immediate needs and developing future updates and improvements. Finan writes, "I can already envision the possibility of this [effort] affecting student retention. Often, yearly updates and program changes are implemented without any feedback from the students we serve. However, planning and implementing an evaluation strategy for important aspects of our program by seeking collaboration with staff and students can help support updates and changes moving forward and ensure they are meaningful for both parties."

Finan's plan highlights several key components of evidence-based teaching. While offering opportunities for evaluation is foundational, it's only one element. Strategies must be developed to use and share the application of discovered data. Applying evidence-based practices in education is crucial as they promote a culture of continuous improvement for both teachers and students. Educators who continually evaluate and fine-tune their teaching strategies set positive examples of flexibility and a growth mindset. Evidence-based teaching improves student achievement, increases engagement, and significantly fuels important social and emotional learning principles.

"When school leaders implement more evidence-based teaching into their system, educators can help ensure students receive high-quality instruction. School improvement leads to student improvement. As teachers strive to help students reach their full potential, schools may also see increases in high school graduation rates, higher college enrollment, and better career outcomes."

— Voyager Sopris Learning

In the *International Journal of Advanced Academic and Educational Research* article, "The Role of Evaluation in Teaching and Learning Process in Education," educator Ehiemere Francisca Ifeoma (2022) summarizes the value of assessment and feedback: "Evaluation is a continuous process and a periodic exercise. It helps in forming the values of judgment, educational status, or achievement of students. Through frequent assessment and feedback, effective teachers regularly assess what they do in the classroom and whether their students are really learning." Ifeoma continues by detailing ten functions of evidence-based practices.

1. **Placement Function:** Evaluation sets a baseline for individualized instruction and provides insight into student learning gaps.

2. **Instructional Function:** Evaluation helps teachers contextualize and improve instruction.

3. **Diagnostic Function:** Evaluation provides the positive and negative feedback required to maintain program strengths and target areas of concern.

4. **Predictive Function:** Evaluation reveals potential abilities and aptitude among the learners that can shape future education and career goals.

5. **Administrative Function:** Evaluation can shape educational policy and decision-making.

6. **Guidance Function:** Evaluation provides necessary educational, vocational, and personal guidance.

7. **Motivational Function:** Evaluation promotes partnership and increases student/teacher buy-in.

8. **Development Function:** Evaluation encourages personal and professional development for all learning community members.

9. **Research Function:** Evaluation provides data useful internally and to education professionals at large.

10. **Communication Function:** Evaluation allows for open discussions about student progress and opportunities to celebrate growth.

In the absence of fact, the human brain attempts to fill in the blanks, leading to assumption and obscured reality. Learning to welcome evaluation-based teaching strategies will not only benefit adult learners but will also assist you, dear educator, in honing your craft and building an environment that genuinely enables the next steps of its students.

Quick Reflection

What areas of your teaching/programming lack routine evaluation? What steps could you take to gather information in that area? How could you use the data collected?

ACTIVITIES AND APPLICATIONS

Now it's your turn! Work through the **Independent Culture Workshop** (see Appendix E) below on your own. Consider partnering with teachers and administrators to evaluate and discuss your results. As the members of the PLC can attest, the insights collected will be invaluable and lay an even stronger foundation for student success and retention.

Culture Checklist:

Select 3 characteristics* of your ideal classroom culture below.
*When describing your class, these are the 3 things you want to be evident.

☐ Collaborative	☐ Autonomous	☐ Friendly	☐ Compassionate	☐ Stimulating
☐ Empathetic	☐ Inclusive	☐ Open	☐ Authentic	☐ Inspirational
☐ Innovative	☐ Productive	☐ Safe	☐ Competitive	☐ Growth-oriented
☐ Motivating	☐ Encouraging	☐ Supportive	☐ Enjoyable	☐ Understanding
☐ Casual	☐ Flexible	☐ Fun	☐ Enlightening	☐ Meaningful

In your own words, define your top 3 cultural traits. What does this characteristic look like?

1.

2.

3.

Culture Evaluation:

Rate* the following statements below.
*Administrators should answer from a programmatic perspective.

My classroom is a safe space.

Definitely, yes!	Kind of	Not so much	Not at all

My classroom has clearly defined academic expectations.

Definitely, yes!	Kind of	Not so much	Not at all

My classroom has clearly defined expectations regarding classroom interactions.

Definitely, yes!	Kind of	Not so much	Not at all

My classroom is physically structured to support ideal culture.

Definitely, yes!	Kind-of	Not so much	Not at all

My classroom models and welcomes valuable feedback.

Definitely, yes!   Kind of   Not so much   Not at all

My classroom implements evaluation-based strategies.

Definitely, yes!   Kind of   Not so much   Not at all

I recognize the life demands of my students.

Definitely, yes!   Kind of   Not so much   Not at all

I know my students' personal goals.

Definitely, yes!   Kind of   Not so much   Not at all

My classroom celebrates student achievement.

Definitely, yes!   Kind of   Not so much   Not at all

My classroom values effort.

Definitely, yes!   Kind of   Not so much   Not at all

Culture Check-In:

Rate* the following statements below.

To be administered to students. See Appendix E, page 161

I feel comfortable asking my teacher questions.

Definitely, yes!   Kind of   Not so much   Not at all

I feel comfortable asking my classmates questions.

Definitely, yes!   Kind of   Not so much   Not at all

I feel comfortable sharing ideas and opinions in my classroom.

Definitely, yes!   Kind of   Not so much   Not at all

I would describe my classroom as a safe space.

Definitely, yes!   Kind of   Not so much   Not at all

Homework and assignments: I understand what is expected of me.

Definitely, yes!   Kind of   Not so much   Not at all

Classroom interactions: I understand what is expected of me.

Definitely, yes!   Kind of   Not so much   Not at all

I always know how I am doing in my studies.

Definitely, yes!   Kind of   Not so much   Not at all

I feel comfortable discussing my work with my teacher.

Definitely, yes!   Kind of   Not so much   Not at all

I feel comfortable discussing my work with other students.

Definitely, yes!   Kind of   Not so much   Not at all

I know what I need to do to make progress.

Definitely, yes!   Kind of   Not so much   Not at all

My teacher knows my life demands outside of class.

Definitely, yes!   Kind of   Not so much   Not at all

My teacher understands my life demands outside of class.

Definitely, yes!   Kind of   Not so much   Not at all

My teacher knows my personal goals.

Definitely, yes!   Kind of   Not so much   Not at all

What are 3 words to describe the perfect classroom?

What are 3 words to describe your current classroom?

Thinking about the statements above, would you like to share anything else?

TOP TAKEAWAYS

Creating Culture: Fostering an Environment for Student Success

- *Ideal classroom culture must be defined.* Educators need to articulate the specific environmental characteristics they want to exemplify and clearly define the culture they want to create.

- *Targeted culture-driven goals create an outline for program improvement.* Student success is supported by specific, purpose-driven objectives.

- *Collective input from all members of a learning community is foundational in establishing culture.* Authentic discussions with staff and students clarify next steps and reinforce programmatic mission and vision.

- *Environments that support student safety must be prioritized.* Feelings of comfort and security in the classroom directly impact student engagement and retention.

- *Contextualized instruction is essential to effective classroom culture.* Adult students thrive in environments that directly link learning to their daily lives and goals.

- *A positive learning environment is powerful!* Caring professionals can shape a learning environment that aids students in advancing their education, developing transferrable skills, and overcoming challenges.

ANCHOR CONNECTION

Are you starting to get the picture? Are you beginning to see how interconnected the Retention Anchors of student retention are?

Use the following questions to note potential connections between retention supporting factors.

How do the first three Retention Anchors connect?

How is culture influenced by the demographic data characterizing adult students?

How can lessons targeted to the just-in-time needs of adult learners support a positive classroom/ program culture?

How could a learning environment be shaped by student/teacher/admin relationships?

How can a culture that encourages a growth mindset aid in measuring student progress?

How can teaching within a thriving and meaningful learning community encourage professional development?

Quick Reflection

Continue to reflect as we investigate new Retention Anchors, and think deeply about the connections between each. Remember, the goal is to create a balanced "retention ship" to maintain and grow student attendance and continuance.

SUPPORT FROM ESSENTIAL EDUCATION

The Essential Education team strives to model a culture of success in everything we do. We build partnerships with administrators, educators, and students founded on the belief that education can change lives. We work to support that belief by creating products and services that embody an exemplary culture's defined, reflective, and growth-oriented nature. We help educators create a culture that supports student success in the following four ways:

Progress monitoring tools that support and celebrate student gains. Essential Education's timely assessments allow educators to continuously measure and celebrate student progress. Students receive immediate feedback and words of encouragement as they advance through lessons and study materials. Motivation and engagement increase when student effort is acknowledged and supported.

Teacher reports that open conversations and create educator-student connections. Our Student Progress Report provides a comprehensive view of individual student gains and learning needs. The data is simple, yet precise and enables educators to give students visual proof of their learning, skill by skill.

LMS messaging features to stay connected to students outside the classroom. Teachers can easily communicate with students collectively or individually within the learning platform. This is a great way to stay in touch throughout the week with reminders and motivational messages.

Dream Catcher to help students explore their purpose and consider next steps. This course seeks to assist students in finding their purpose, setting goals, and creating a roadmap for personal success. Classroom culture is improved when goals are set and shared. Academic effort and achievements are given greater value when tied to larger student aspirations.

GETTING
CONNECTED

CREATING RELATIONSHIPS
FOR CONTINUANCE

REVIEWING THE RESEARCH

The human brain is complex. While it may be tempting to believe that learning is fully based on the ability to process information, neurological function is much more intricate. An adult student's academic success is not solely based on their capacity to recall details, apply new knowledge, or solve problems. Feelings of comfort, acceptance, and encouragement are the dopamine-infused fuel for the motivation, resilience, and confidence required to learn and grow.

"We are not thinking machines that feel; rather, we are feeling machines that think."

—Antonio Damasio, University of Southern California

We've discussed a bit of this truth in previous Retention Anchors. To learn *who* adult students are, we must look beyond statistics on a page and delve into personal values, needs, and goals. As we tailor what we teach, we must consider ways to boost student excitement and engagement. Even *where* we teach is strongly influenced by how students feel about their learning environment. It's no surprise, as we further address how to better meet student needs and improve continuance, that we anchor ourselves in yet another feelings-driven element: relationships.

Relationships are the "glue" of student retention, because they hold all other retention influencing factors together. They are the "how" of the Retention Anchors. How do we get to know our adult students? Relationships. How do we customize instruction based on student interests and career paths? Relationships. How do we foster an environment that encourages students to take their next step? Relationships. Relationships are the connecting component of every Anchor discussed thus far and will be a key element of those yet to be explored. But why relationships?

Take a few moments and use the space below to write a few reflections.

Why are school-based relationships so pivotal to student success?

What types of relationships should be considered?

Do relationships impact how or what you teach?

How do relationships shape your current classroom environment?

How has your personal academic journey been shaped by relationships?

When discussing academic interactions, most will immediately think about the connections between students and teachers. After all, strong student-teacher relationships are a crucial element in effective and efficient learning. When students feel known and cared for by their teacher, they have a greater sense of accountability, are more comfortable asking questions, and possess the confidence required to take risks and effectively master new skills. Learning is more efficient because students feel less isolated. When students feel supported by their teachers, they are less likely to fear embarrassment or criticism. Teachers who intentionally invest in building relationships create a proverbial safety net for students. Whether viewed as a guide or a sage, educators who commit to establishing strong student connections can significantly impact student growth and academic progress. Students want to attend class when they are seen, respected, and making strides toward their individual goals. Retention rates improve when student-teacher relationships are prioritized.

"Students are more likely to learn when they feel cared for and valued by their teacher. Students tend to be more motivated to learn and be engaged in the classroom when their teacher likes and cares about them."

—Christi Bergin, University of Missouri

"Building rapport with your students and establishing yourself as their mentor is an excellent way to combat chronic absenteeism. Students are more motivated to attend classes if they know their teacher cares about them and will help them succeed."

—Waterford

Studies further show that students are not the only ones who benefit from solid student-teacher relationships. Teachers also reap the rewards of positive interactions with students. A 2022 study at the University of Missouri found positive student-teacher relationships resulted in improved instruction. Christi Bergin, Associate Dean and lead author on the study, notes, "Positive teacher-student relationships change student behavior, and in this study, we found building those positive relationships actually leads to better teaching, too. It changes teacher behavior." (University of Missouri, 2022). Bergin discovered that students who indicated strong relationships with their teachers also reported the use of more high-impact teaching practices.

Research goes on to note that teacher retention also increases when teachers establish strong bonds with their students. Just as students are encouraged when their study efforts yield academic progress, teachers are encouraged when their instruction leads to the growth and success of their students.

The circular nature of the student-teacher relationship (Figure 4.1) is important to note. As students build mentoring connections with educators, motivation improves, and progress is boosted. As teachers build these relationships, they can better individualize and contextualize instruction. Improved instruction leads to better student outcomes and helps students see the value of their efforts. This realization further strengthens the trust they have in their teacher. The teacher takes pride in a job well done, and the benefit cycle continues. Student progress and program continuance are closely intertwined with teacher effectiveness and educator retention.

"Building positive relationships with students can help teachers, too. 25-40% of new teachers are likely to leave the education field within five years. But positive relationships with students can reduce this number and show teachers how their career changes lives."

—Waterford

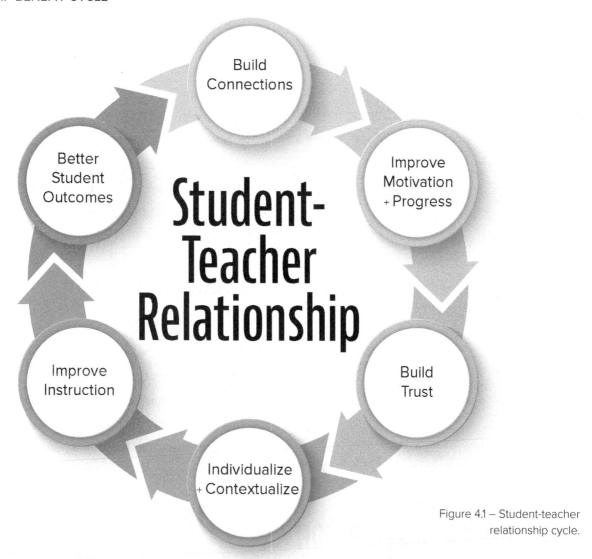

Figure 4.1 – Student-teacher relationship cycle.

The power of student-teacher interactions is well-documented. But are these interactions the only connections impacting retention? Relationships are multifaceted. Each of us has a number of significant interpersonal connections, and these relationships shape who we are and what we do. In Retention Anchor 3, we discussed the mirroring effect that occurs when we spend considerable time with a specific person or group of people. We begin to emulate the behavior of others and fall into a series of social norms and patterns. So how do these connections impact student retention?

The diversity of the adult education classroom lends itself to a variety of influential relationships beyond the student-teacher bond. Two of the most notable are student-student relationships and teacher-teacher relationships. Though often less discussed than student-teacher connections, these relationships can have a significant impact on student motivation, classroom retention, and program completion. Let's spend some time focusing on these relationship types and examine their effect on classroom attendance and continuance.

Quick Reflection

Have you ever considered how peer relationships in the classroom affect retention? In what ways could strong teacher-teacher relationships combat chronic absenteeism?

EVALUATION AND REFLECTION

To learn more about the power of student-student and teacher-teacher connections and their impact on retention, we once again enlisted the help of Essential Education's Professional Learning Community (PLC). We asked PLC educators and administrators to research the strength of peer and colleague relationships as a catalyst for student continuance. They were instructed to evaluate student-student and teacher-teacher relationships within their programs and create an activity or series of activities to strengthen those connections. Their findings were enlightening and encouraging and provided a number of practical applications.

As we detail their research and initiatives, consider the student-student and teacher-teacher relationships in your organization. Are these connections intentionally addressed and cultivated? What are some areas of relational strength? Which relationships could use extra time and attention? Take a few notes as you read and reflect on how some of the PLC activities could be tailored to boost peer and colleague interactions at your site.

Student-Student Relationships

Peer collaboration and student progress often tightly align in the classroom. Previous Retention Anchors have noted that the relationships adult students have with their classmates can increase feelings of comfort and safety, improve accountability, and play a significant role in shaping a positive classroom environment.

PLC educator Ester Garcia used the results of the **Independent Culture Workshop** (see Appendix E) presented in Retention Anchor 3 as a springboard for learning more about the student-student interactions at Cory Learning Center in Odessa, Texas. She writes, "After collecting as much data as I could from the students that attend regularly, I found that quite a few students replied 'kind of' when asked about [positively] interacting with their classmates. I hoped that they would all get to know one another on their own, and some have, but there are still some that are shy and not social. I want to bridge that gap between the students and hopefully turn those 'kind of' responses into 'definitely yes' replies."

"Research suggests that positive peer relationships are associated with better school engagement – including increased attendance and classroom participation – and can help build students' sense of belonging."

—Transforming Education

"In a positive learning environment, students lift one another up and create an atmosphere where it is the norm to take risks, ask questions, make mistakes, and learn collaboratively. In order to set the stage for this type of environment, students not only need a good relationship with their teacher, they need to feel connected to their peers."

—Jill Fletcher, Edutopia

Meet Your Classmates

To address the need for stronger peer relationships, Garcia organized a *Meet Your Classmates* event offered at two separate times known to be most convenient for the students. Garcia urged online learners and those who pick up and drop off homework packets to attend in person as well. The program director provided snacks and resources for the gatherings.

As students entered the meet-up, they were greeted and given a few icebreaker activities. An **All About Me** **Exercise** (see Appendix F) encouraged students to share more about themselves. The intro questions were simple and light. Students were asked about their families, pets, hobbies, favorite foods, colors, movies, and sports teams. They were also asked to note a few dislikes. Questions toward the end of the activity inquired about previous school experiences, career goals, and personal motivators. Garcia provided examples of the questions asked in the exercise.

Garcia opened the discussion by personally answering a few of the starter questions in the exercise and encouraged students to do the same. Her comfort in sharing gave students the confidence to join in the discussion. As the depth of the questions progressed, so did the responses. Students found common ground in their interests and career goals. Many openly discussed the obstacles they face as adult students. Garcia detailed her own story of why she became an adult educator and expressed her care and commitment to student success. In detailing her "why," the students revealed more about what inspires them to keep pursuing their goals.

The sense of unity, ease, and connectedness was evident. Several students noted a shift in the "vibe" of the group and discussed plans for future events. Garcia closed their time together by thanking the students for attending, acknowledging their busy schedules, and expressing her appreciation for spending some of their valuable time getting to know other adult learners.

The next day, students were given the opportunity to reflect on the *Meet Your Classmates* activity. Those in attendance collectively agreed the event was welcoming and fun. They thoroughly enjoyed meeting other students and learning more about each other's lives and hopes for the future. Some noted an intent to attend more tutoring sessions because they appreciated the time shared with learners facing similar obstacles. Others conveyed gratitude for the program's strong support system and the encouraging connections they are making with their classmates. In the middle of their discussion, Garcia received a phone call from a student who could not attend. With the student's permission, she shared the details of their conversation.

PLC Conversation: Ester Garcia

"She called to excuse herself. I assured her that it was fine and that I would catch her up when she made it in. She went on to tell me that she had lost her mother to domestic violence the night before. I set my "teacher" voice aside and used my

"comfort" voice. I shared with the students in attendance {that} I was astounded that she would call. A student said 'Ms., you are our safe space. That girl needed to hear your voice to let her know she would be okay.' This student was told that we (myself and her classmates) were here for her should she need anything. She was very thankful. We all just sighed as a group and discovered that we do not know what others are going through outside of our classroom."

Garcia concluded her reflection by stating, "We can provide all the tools and remove as many barriers that we can to help adult learners, but we cannot control their lives outside of the classroom. So we show up for those that show up."

Coffee and Me Too!

PLC educator Susan Spradlin also chose to target student-student relationships in her classes at Tennessee College of Applied Technology-Knoxville. Spradlin, however, faced an added challenge. Her classes are completely virtual. While her shift to teaching online has impacted multiple areas of instruction, deepening student connections virtually has been exceptionally difficult. The task ahead called for courage and creativity. She needed to step out of her own comfort zone and try something new.

Spradlin designed an activity called Coffee and Me Too! Students were invited to a "morning meeting" and asked to bring coffee, tea, or any other breakfast beverage before logging on. They were also asked to think of something about themselves to share with the group. Responses could be anything they felt comfortable conveying. They could talk about their favorite foods, family, pets, movies, or music they like. Spradlin kicked off the conversation by inviting students to relax and enjoy their coffee while she shared a few things about herself. She then encouraged the students to discuss their favorite things or something they enjoy.

Sensing that some students may be reluctant to participate, Spradlin explained the "me too" component of the activity. As each student read their statement, the other students were asked to shout out, type in the chat, or use a symbol to signify, "Hey, me too!" if they agreed or could identify with what was shared. She also prepared some sample statements to keep the conversation flowing. "I started with, 'My favorite pet is a dog.' There were a couple of "me toos." But one student replied, 'No way, cats are much cooler.' [Another] student said, "I think Outlander is the dumbest show ever." There were gasps as no one could say, 'Me too.' However, that started a 15-minute conversation on binging Netflix shows, the good and bad, and the pros and cons of watching too much TV in general. So I consider that a win!"

The activity continued until all students had a chance to share or react to the other students' statements. In reflecting on the retention connection within the exercise, Spradlin shared the following.

> *"When students connect with others and can find common ground, they will return to class to see their 'friends.' They may even find enough of a connection to exchange emails or phone numbers and talk outside of class."*

—Susan Spradlin, Tennessee College of Applied Technology

Coffee and Me Too! has become a monthly part of Spradlin's classroom routine. In addition to encouraging class attendance and program retention, she also hopes to see budding peer relationships evolve into mentoring opportunities. She writes, "The bigger picture idea was to show [students] they are not alone. I wanted them to make connections to other folks navigating the same study habits or challenges and maybe struggling with the same content. I think when people realize they have something in common with someone, even something as small as a favorite animal/pet, that it is the very beginning of making meaningful connections and deepening relationships, even over a computer screen."

Motivation and Goal Setting

Online instructors are not the only sector of educators facing unique barriers to building student-student relationships. Corrections institutions also have to think creatively about how to best build and leverage peer relationships for academic success and program completion. In facing this distinct challenge, PLC contributor and corrections educator, LaDonna Torrey tapped into her earlier discoveries within our retention studies. Having already instituted measures to better understand her students and promote a culture of goal setting, Torrey hoped to build on this framework to establish stronger connections among students.

Utilizing short motivational videos aligned to specific student goals, Torrey implemented a series of lessons designed to encourage students to think deeply about personal motivations and aspirations. She noted that highlighting the personal nature of goal setting and academic achievement is especially difficult but imperative for her students to succeed. "The culture of incarceration is that they belong to a gang and are finding their rank. In class, I am asking them to get motivated to be individuals and [become] the best they can be for themselves." Ironically, prompting students to look inward resulted in them outwardly engaging with other students.

Torrey states, "I had a student willing to open up and share his goals. This allowed the class to connect in a way they never had before. It also allowed the class to see how [their] lives are not so different. When class started, the ice was broken, and communication was open. Using a motivation and goal setting system [is] building a community."

The students found commonality in several pivotal success factors. Many agreed that self-discipline, not being defined by your past, and opportunities for a brighter future were shared drivers. When asked to consider healthy sources of peer connection, many discovered there are multiple resources for support within their institution. Opportunities to connect in the classroom, dorms, and recreational communities were all noted as positive alternatives to the divisive and sometimes dangerous group dynamics within the prison system. The students also compiled a list of things to help them stay accountable in their studies. They indicated completing homework, tracking test scores, and consistently attending class as important elements in achieving their goals.

Torrey is pleased to report that encouraging students to focus on their future and the people or things that push them to look beyond their current circumstances has dramatically improved program retention. Her students are beginning to see life through a different lens. The comfort level in the classroom has shifted. There is a greater sense of belonging, and a more positive, inclusive learning environment is being established.

In addition to the PLC student-student relationship builders, here are a few additional activities to encourage classmate connections.

- **Plan group learning activities.** Working together to solve a problem or complete group projects is a terrific way for students to connect. Working toward a common goal strengthens relationships.

- **Create shared interest initiatives.** Consider grouping students with common career interests when working through content specific to a particular job or field. Reading materials customized to personal interests are known to boost engagement. Add a relational component by uniting learners with mutual aspirations.

- **Open group discussions.** Subject discussions encourage new ideas and problem-solving techniques. When students feel heard and understood by their peers, connections deepen.

- **Share success stories.** Adult students need to hear from others who have overcome the challenges they are currently facing. Inspiration and confidence are increased as successful learners say, "If I can do it, so can you!"

- **Embrace brain breaks.** Have fun! Just a few moments of downtime allow students to take a collective breath and interact with each other. Investing a bit of time in casual conversation can have a big impact on the classroom atmosphere. Remember, mood is a known ingredient in creating "Aha!" moments.

Quick Reflection

Which discoveries within the PLC findings and suggested activities to build peer connections stand out to you? Which exercises could be most beneficial for your students? Can you think of ways to customize some of these ideas to build a student-student community in your classroom or program?

Teacher-Teacher Relationships

Now, let's examine another type of relationship crucial to student retention: the teacher-teacher relationship. We've already established the powerful influence student-teacher connections can have on quality instruction by promoting student engagement. How, then, does the relationship between educators themselves improve teaching and student success?

In the same way that student-student relationships provide support and encouragement for learners, positive teacher-teacher connections can significantly impact educator morale and performance. Adult educators share distinct motivations and struggles, but they are largely united in purpose. Fueled by the desire to change lives through learning, teacher-teacher relationships can provide empathetic encouragement, improve instructional effectiveness, combat fatigue, and strengthen commitment to the profession. Just as students need support from their peers to grow, teachers need connection with their colleagues to thrive.

"When teachers perceive their colleagues as compassionate towards them, they show higher levels of organizational commitment, positive emotion, and job satisfaction; they are also better able to cope with stress and less likely to experience burnout."

— Greater Good in Education

Teacher-teacher relationships not only benefit educators but also improve student outcomes. A 2021 study from the *Asian Journal of University Education* titled "Can Teacher Collaboration Improve Students' Academic Achievement in Junior Secondary Mathematics?" highlighted the advantages of teacher-teacher connections and their positive impact on students. The study in question conducted a comparative analysis of academic performance in mathematics among secondary students in Nigeria (Saka, 2021). The comparison focused on students taught by teachers who actively collaborated with colleagues and those taught by teachers working independently. The findings established a direct correlation between teacher collaboration and student achievement. Data showed that students whose teachers worked with other teachers to plan instruction performed better than those taught by a teacher who did not engage in collaboration.

Teacher collaboration also fosters an environment of positive professional development where educators can embrace, respect, and learn from the experiences of other instructors. Through collaborative endeavors, teachers tap into the expertise of their colleagues. Teacher-teacher relationships encourage educators to reflect on their classroom methodologies, participate in productive dialogue, and welcome the exchange of ideas. These interactions build solid working relationships among the faculty. Peer observation and feedback are less intimidating and more effective when strong teacher bonds are formed. Educators are encouraged to hone their craft and create dynamic learning experiences for students. When the student experience is enhanced, increased engagement and improved classroom attendance follow suit.

"Effective teacher to teacher communication is vitally essential to your success as a teacher. Regular collaboration and team planning sessions are extremely valuable. Engaging in these practices has a positive impact on teacher effectiveness."

— Derrick Meador, ThoughtCo.

`Get-to-Know-Me

As PLC educators examined the role teacher-teacher relationships have in retention, they reached similar conclusions. Many also discovered that some of the same types of activities that boost student-student connections are also helpful in building positive teacher-teacher interactions.

Adult educator and PLC contributor Kelly Grudowski shared an activity she created and implemented as an adult education administrator. In the program's first staff meeting, a *Get-to-Know-Me* slide show highlighting fun facts about each staff member was shared with the team. Similar to the *Meet Your Classmates* and *Coffee and Me Too!* activities created for students, she asked teachers to share a few of their favorite things, interests, and hobbies. Staff members submitted contributions to Grudowski in advance, and she compiled the responses into an interactive presentation.

She shared, "The activity opened great communication. We asked and answered questions with each other. We commented on some of the things we had in common. We learned some new information about each other. Even though this activity was simple, it opened up great dialogue and allowed the team to feel connected."

Grudowski also emphasized the importance of recognizing all program staff as contributors to student success. "My staff is more than teachers. When all staff members like and respect one another, students definitely see and feel that. Our culture is healthier. As the year goes on, I plan to use team building activities to grow our relationships so our students benefit from the positive environment."

Echoing the power of simple, fun activities to strengthen effective teacher-teacher relationships, Christina Smith, an adult educator and PLC contributor from Goodwill Gulf Coast, shared her team's recent experience at an adult education conference. She noted that the purpose of the trip was professional development, but many bonds formed after the daily conference sessions ended. She writes, "We recently took a trip to Birmingham for a conference. This was my first one as I am the newest of my team. At the first night mixer, I fearlessly sang Karaoke and surprised my colleagues. That was the first time outside of work that we got to just hang out. We [had] two days of professional training. At the end of each day, over dinner, we discussed and shared what we had learned that day. Even later, we stayed up in the lobby and enjoyed each other's company. This trip was a great opportunity to learn more about my colleagues who are not just my coworkers but are now close friends."

Smith says, "The importance of teacher-teacher relationships extends beyond the classroom. Supportive relationships among educators create a positive work environment, which in turn increases job satisfaction and reduces burnout. Collaborative relationships foster a sense of belonging, camaraderie, and empathy among teachers. This support network allows teachers to share successes and challenges, seek advice, and receive constructive feedback."

Virtual Brainstorm and Debrief

Cherie Goranites, PLC educator and administrator at Bonny Eagle Adult Education in Maine, opted to address two retention-impacting relationships simultaneously. She developed a pre-term opportunity for her teachers to learn more about their students while at the same time collaborating as a group. Her efforts intended to establish a foundation for student-teacher relationships and enhance teacher-teacher connections.

Goranites kickstarted the initiative with a *Virtual Brainstorm*. Recognizing and honoring the time commitments of her part-time instructors, she chose to conduct the session in an online environment at a time convenient for most of her staff. During the meet-up, educators were encouraged to share their goals, plans, and hopes for the upcoming semester. To personalize their discussions, Goranites provided a **Student Information Table** (see Appendix G). The chart, shown below, was pre-populated with information collected during the program's intake process. The data provided teachers with valuable details about their incoming students, including preferred names, goals, educational backgrounds, perceived learning styles, and current test scores.

Using the demographic information provided in the table, instructors created a few get-to-know-you activities to use at the beginning of the next school term. Goranites provided a few suggestions to get them started. She also supplied a template letter addressed to students that each teacher could customize. This letter expressed the program's desire to individualize instruction and create a supportive learning environment for all adult learners.

At the end of the first week of classes, Goranites gathered instructors for a *Virtual Debrief*. Each instructor shared what they learned from the get-to-know-you activities conducted with their students. They combined their findings with the information provided in the *Student Information Table* in an effort to identify students of particular need. Goranites also asked the teachers to create an "exit slip" noting what worked well with these activities and what could be improved.

Upon reflection, Goranites writes, "After reviewing the input provided in the exit slips, I would say this experiment went well and met the main goal

Student Chart:

To be completed for incoming students.

Student's Name	Gender / Pronouns	Brief Description of Student's Educational Background	Goals	Learning Style *(Visual, Auditory, or Tactile)*	HA Math Practice Test Score	HA Reading Practice Test Score	HA Writing Practice Test Score

of helping teachers to feel connected and learn from each other. Our part-time instructors were actually quite eager to participate in the project's activities. They immediately replied to my emails asking for their participation, and we had zero issues finding times to hold our meetings. In some ways, I felt like I was offering them an opportunity that they had been waiting for."

She notes that the *Student Information Table* was extremely helpful for the instructors. While the information had always been provided in student files, score reports, and enrollment forms, the table organizes the data in a short, user-friendly format. When information is easy to digest, data-driven instruction is more manageable, efficient, and targeted. It is precisely that type of targeted instruction that seeks to keep students in class and on track for success.

Goranites intends to continue to hold virtual and in-person opportunities for teachers throughout the semester. Educators will be encouraged to review updated student data, discuss student progress, and share ideas to improve instruction. She hopes that by providing these opportunities to connect, a stronger network of support can be established for teachers and students alike.

As our study on the importance of teacher collaboration continued, one key barrier continued to rise to the surface: time. While all agreed relationships between colleagues are valuable, the already demanding schedules of educators present a significant challenge. A recent survey reported that only 31% of teachers have enough time to collaborate with other teachers, and 4% said that they never meet with other teachers to discuss student success or instruction. The time constraints are real,

but greater collaboration among educators is possible with intention, creativity, and planning.

More Teacher Connections

Our PLC administrators have already provided a few wonderful examples showing how to cultivate teacher-teacher relationships. Virtual meetings are extremely helpful in integrating collaboration into the busy lives of adult educators. Providing time and resources for professional conferences is another investment that reaps a multitude of rewards.

Here are a few more ideas for teachers and administrators striving to build and bolster teacher connections.

- **Schedule student-free planning days.** Planning instruction in the midst of delivering instruction is common for many educators. Providing opportunities for teachers to solely focus on evaluating and preparing lessons when students are not in class allows for greater focus and group collaboration.

- **Find time for fun.** Enlist the help of an internal planning committee to organize out-of-class social opportunities for staff. Create a positive work environment by making social relationships among educators a priority.

- **Plan with purpose.** Carve out common time for teacher teams to meet and focus on one targeted initiative (i.e., plan a specific lesson, tackle a certain standard or skill, or address one area of program improvement). Educators feel a greater sense of accomplishment when they attack a singular problem as a group and devise a practical solution.

- **Observe with an objective.** Work with teachers to schedule classroom visits that address developing skills. Pair educators appropriately by matching teachers with strong techniques with educators in need of specific strategies.

- **Make room for messaging.** Use voice tools like Voxer, Marco Polo, Zoom Chat, Slack, or Microsoft Teams for quick communication.

- **Create a collaboration space.** Tap into free resources like Jamboard and Padlet. Build discussion topics and questions that allow teachers to add thoughts and suggestions on the go.

- **Utilize social media communities.** Expand your teacher network by learning from a wider range of professionals. Share insights and discuss new findings with local program educators.

- **Invest in professional training.** As resources allow, encourage educators to continue their education. While some opportunities require monetary support and travel, there are a number of professional development opportunities offered online and in person at little to no cost. These offerings not only enhance teaching skills but they strengthen valuable educator connections.

Quick Reflection

List additional ideas for building teacher-teacher relationships.

ACTIVITIES AND APPLICATIONS

As we've discussed and worked through the dynamics of student-teacher, student-student, and teacher-teacher relationships, have you noticed any common themes or strategies? Have you noticed the similarities between the activities and suggestions within the text? Did you note just how many of the PLC projects revolved around asking and answering questions? Could the key to building effective relationships in the classroom center around one pivotal element?

Studies show that first impressions are made in just seven seconds. Whether meeting new friends, classmates, or coworkers, those first few moments of interaction are critical. But a gut reaction is not a quality basis for establishing a real connection. Initial impressions are based largely on assumptions. Real connections seek the truth. Relationships are based on curiosity.

 ## *Curiosity is powerful.*

It pushes us to question ourselves, our world, and our current circumstances. The curious mind thinks critically, solves problems, and seeks creative solutions. Curious people are change-makers. Relationally curious people build connections that dip beneath the surface of first impressions and push past assumptions. What else do we know about curiosity?

 ## *Curious people are present.*

They see details that are easily missed and ask, "Why?" Why is one particular student always late? Why is a typically happy student now distant and discouraged? Why do certain students seem to be mastering concepts in class but perform poorly on exams? Why is one type of instruction helpful for one student but not another? Why do some educators seem to be more effective than others? Being alert and attentive to detail is crucial to identifying needs and facilitating growth and change.

 ## *Curious people take risks.*

Many of our PLC educators discovered stepping out of their own comfort zones and encouraging others to do the same to be a huge catalyst for jumpstarting relationships. Trying something new, sharing personal stories or life experiences, or opening up about challenges, struggles, and goals breaks down walls. Like calls to like. People find comfort, encouragement, and inspiration in shared struggles and triumphs.

 ## *Curious people ask questions.*

If you do not know, you cannot grow. Questions provide information. Questions allow for reflection. Questions spur new ideas and relay insights about others that could easily remain hidden. Questions matter and are vital to making meaningful connections.

So we challenge you, fellow educators. Be curious! We've provided a tool to help spark your curious nature. Our **Curiosity = Connection Question Generator** (see Appendix H) is designed to help you develop curiosity and strengthen success-driven relationships. The questions listed are a jumping-off point and can be customized to address student-teacher, student-student, and teacher-teacher connections. We trust they will inspire you to develop your own activities to strengthen retention-yielding relationships in your classroom or program.

Additional Support

Essential Education's *3D Differentiation Guide* (https://bit.ly/410MOPA) is a powerful resource for this Retention Anchor and helps educators plan and create engaging instruction for all learners. Many of the suggested activities serve more than one purpose. Consider how you can implement a few of these exercises (Figures 4.2–4.5) to cultivate continuance-strengthening connections in your program.

DISTANCE LEARNING EXERCISES

To Be Honest
Briefly explain the upcoming unit of study and ask students to write three truth statements about that topic. You will discover very quickly how individual students feel about a given area of study. They may reveal past struggles, display confidence in a given area, or expose their like/dislike for a given topic. Student responses may provide valuable insight into how to deliver new information.

Figure 4.2 – From *Discover: Evaluate Student Needs*, pg. 17

Finish the Sentence
Compose a short set of sentences to be completed by each student. I am happiest when _____. A perfect day would be _____. If I could go anywhere in the world, it would be _____. These could be completed as one activity with a given group of students or given one sentence at a time as students arrive.

Figure 4.3 – From *Discover: Evaluate Student Needs*, pg. 17

If I Wrote the Test
In classrooms targeted to high school equivalency test prep, ask students what they would put on the exam if they were in charge. In other words, what do they think are the minimum skills everyone should possess. The answers may surprise you and will provide a peek into student value systems.

Figure 4.4 – From *Discover: Evaluate Student Needs*, pg. 17

Likes/Dislikes
Build a student questionnaire of preferences regarding school and learning. I like to learn by _____. I dislike when teachers _____. I like to study (by myself/in a group/a little of both). My favorite school memory is _____. My least favorite memory is _____. My favorite subject is _____. My least favorite subject is _____. Stress honestly and prepare yourself for the responses!

Figure 4.5 – From *Discover: Evaluate Student Needs*, pg. 18

TOP TAKEAWAYS

Getting Connected: Creating Relationships for Continuance

- *Relationships are the "glue" of student retention.* Personal connections hold all other retention influencing factors together.

- *Students excel with they feel known and cared for by their teacher.* They have a greater sense of accountability, are more comfortable asking questions, and possess the confidence to take risks and effectively master new skills.

- *Positive student-teacher relationships improve instruction.* Learning is supported by a strong foundation of trust and accountability.

- *Classroom connections support educator longevity.* Teacher retention also increases when teachers establish strong bonds with their students.

- *Peer collaboration and student progress are tightly aligned.* Adult students' relationships with their classmates can increase feelings of comfort and safety, improve accountability, and create a more supportive learning environment.

- *Educator collaboration is powerful.* Teacher-teacher relationships encourage educators to reflect on their classroom methodologies, participate in productive dialogue, and welcome the exchange of ideas.

ANCHOR CONNECTION

Use the following questions to note potential connections between Retention Anchors.

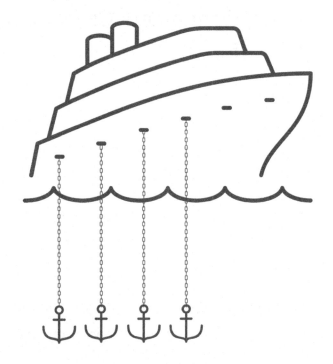

The intro to this Retention Anchor described relationships as the "glue" of student retention. What does that mean to you? How do the first four Retention Anchors connect?

How are relationships influenced by the demographic data characterizing adult students?

How can lessons targeted to the just-in-time needs of adult learners strengthen classroom relationships?

How do student-teacher and student-student relationships shape the learning environment?

How can relationships aid in creating a culture that encourages a growth mindset?

How can tracking and measuring student progress be supported by strong relationships?

What role do relationships play in educator professional development?

SUPPORT FROM ESSENTIAL EDUCATION

Essential Education is here to support educator endeavors to build strong classroom connections that improve student retention. Our product features and program offerings assist in strengthening the communication and curiosity required to build healthy school-based relationships in the following ways:

Internal messaging features. Teachers and administrators can communicate with students and other users directly through our robust learning management system. Correspondence can be sent to an entire class, a specific group, or to individual students. Messaging can add clarity to assignments and provide valuable feedback.

Robust reporting features. Our student progress reports provide a visual representation of student growth. These reports can guide meaningful conversations between teachers and students about learning objectives and skill mastery.

Time-conscious professional development. Essential Education offers a wide array of easy-to-access, live, and on-demand sources of professional development to promote teacher interaction and collaboration. Discover new approaches in adult education, training specific to implementing Essential Education, personalized training, and more!

MEASURING PROGRESS

TRACKING, IMPROVING, AND CELEBRATING GAINS

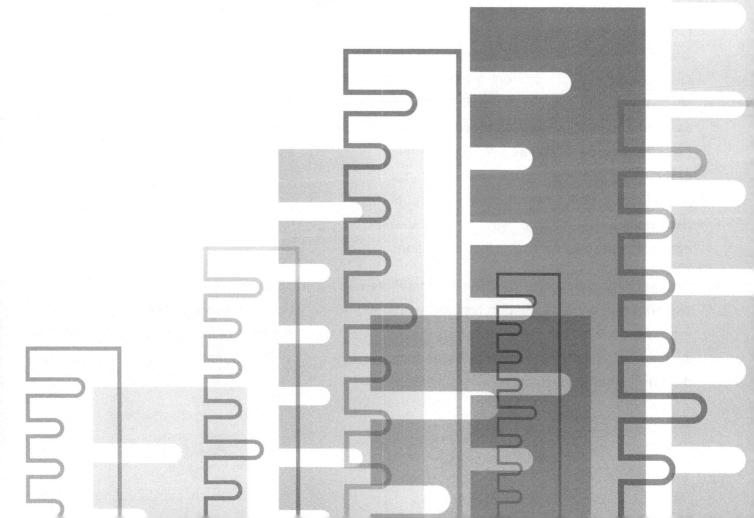

REVIEWING THE RESEARCH

Why do you do what you do? Let's clarify. Why, fellow educators, do you choose to serve in adult education? Is it to make a difference? See others succeed? Maybe you hope to boost student confidence or open doors to opportunity. Do you want to change lives, help students gain independence, or find their life's purpose? Perhaps it's all of the above. Perhaps it's something entirely different.

In previous Retention Anchors, we took a nod from best practices in business and manufacturing and attempted to articulate what we hope to "produce" in adult education. We collectively defined that objective as supporting "people capable of taking their next step." It's a broad yet inclusive definition, as those "next steps" differ for each student. Each has different dreams, long-range goals, and aspirations. Each student has different immediate needs and academic hurdles. Our students navigate different responsibilities, life demands, and personal challenges. Progress varies from learner to learner in speed, accuracy, and effectiveness. There are different timelines, benchmarks, short-term goals, and long-range plans. Each student's next step differs because each student has a unique "why." Why did they enroll? Why are they continuing their education?

Quick Reflection

Why are you an adult educator? Respond below in your own words.

Progress is the "why" of the Retention Anchors. Once we have a greater understanding of *who* our students are, *what* type of instruction best fits their needs, and develop a plan for *where* and *how* we will support them, we move on to helping students progress toward their next step. Ultimately our "why" is helping students fulfill their "why." Their "why" is the source of motivation, resilience, and class attendance. Without the "why," there is no retention.

EVALUATION AND REFLECTION

Take a moment to reflect on these questions here before moving forward.

How do we know if we are accomplishing our objective?

How do we know they are working toward their why?

How do we know students are learning?

How do we know they are making progress?

Measuring Progress

Some markers of student progress are tangible. They can be seen. Scores, grades, and performance-based evidence of growth are common indicators of "student success." So how can educators best evaluate student progress through quantitative data? Many turn to formal assessments like quizzes and tests. Others look to high school equivalency exercises and certification exams. Some may compare student performance to a series of program, state, or national standards. This data is critical in monitoring student improvement and providing evidence of program effectiveness.

The sources of quantitative data in adult education differ significantly among organizations, schools, and programs. Teachers preparing students for the Test of Adult Basic Education (TABE) and the Comprehensive Adult Student Assessment Systems (CASAS) tests have a different set of benchmarks than organizations helping students pass their high school equivalency (HSE) exams. Programs supporting English as a Second Language (ESL) learners and English Speakers of Other Languages (ESOL) students have distinct success markers as well. A program's affiliation, funding source, and curricular structure provide the formal framework used to measure quantitative student progress.

"Quantitative data is, quite simply, information that can be quantified. It can be counted or measured and given a numerical value. If you have questions such as 'How many?', 'How often?' or 'How much?' you'll find the answers in quantitative data."

— Emily Stevens, Career Foundry

"Education research often relies on the quantitative methodology. Quantitative research in education provides numerical data that can prove or disprove a theory, and administrators can easily share the number-based results with other schools and districts."

— American University School of Education

The National Reporting System for Adult Education (NRS) strives to collectively analyze this data in the form of Measurable Skill Gains (MSGs). Students typically display a skill gain when they advance one NRS/Educational Functioning Level (EFL) or earn a secondary school diploma. Students included in the data must be enrolled in a certified adult education program and complete at least 40 hours of instruction between tracked assessments. NRS data is reported annually and can be broken down by individual standards and a number of skill development factors. For more information about NRS data and a deeper understanding of adult student EFL levels, access our Measuring Progress Webinar Handout (see Appendix I).

Some indicators of progress, however, are less visible or lack the ability to be measured with precision. Student effort, improved motivation, or greater ease in tackling a specific problem aren't as visible as a number on a page. Yet these qualitative signs of progress are no less valuable. Consider the student who was previously dedicating one night per week to study and now invests three evenings. That's progress. Perhaps a student who previously struggled with articulating the main idea of a passage is now clearly conveying their own thoughts in writing. That's progress. Maybe someone who became easily frustrated and resisted sharing answers in class is now openly taking risks and continuing to try. That's progress as well.

"Qualitative data plays a crucial role in education as it provides insights into complex phenomena that quantitative data alone cannot capture. While quantitative data can provide information about student performance and achievement, it does not provide a complete picture of the factors that influence these outcomes."

—Innovare

"While quantitative data frequently grabs the spotlight, its qualitative counterpart is just as important for understanding how complicated learning environments work."

—Harshad Deshpande, QuestionPro

In truth, educators need to attune themselves to both quantitative and qualitative measures of progress. Multiple indicators of growth provide teachers and administrators with a clearer picture of where an adult student is, where they hope to go, and what support the student will need to get them there.

"It is essential when considering evaluation that the core purpose is the collection of data that informs us on how best to aid our students in learning and, more specifically, learning the skills they need to reach their specific goals. At times, we tend to consider too much the false dichotomy of quantitative versus qualitative data rather than understanding that both forms of assessments provide us with valuable pieces that can round out our creation of instructional goals and priorities."

—Lyle Ring, Briya Public Charter School

While there are differing methodologies, approaches, and opinions on measuring progress in adult education, educators tend to agree on three essential truths.

1. **There is room for improvement.**

    The MSG data reported by NRS in the last three years places average national skills gains in the mid-30th percentile. There is clearly work to be done. Although this data may appear daunting, we must continue to be diligent in our pursuit of excellence. We must continue to seek innovative solutions to improve instruction and student engagement.

2. **Adult student progress is complex.**

    State and national performance rates are just one part of the puzzle that is adult education. Students need to meet certain standards. Certifications are linked to performance. Test scores matter. However, they are not a full indicator of student progress or teacher effectiveness. The growth mindset we attempt to frame for our students must continue to highlight the incremental nature of success.

3. **Progress requires retention.**

    The formula is simple. Students must be present to learn, exercise, and master new content and skills. The time spent in class and independent study directly correlates to student progress. While some students may require more or less time than others, the connection between time and progress cannot be severed. Seat time leads to success.

Tracking Progress

Setting and tracking progress toward goals is important for all learners. However, adult students, in particular, benefit from a progress-tracking system. Adult learners need to know their efforts are paying off. They need to see the results of their labor. Adult educators must access student data to customize instruction and home in on individual strengths and needs.

The tools available to track student progress are abundant. Some are predetermined by program administrators, interwoven into curricular resources, or individualized by teachers to fit instructional needs. Online applications, spreadsheets, journals, observations, surveys, personal reflections, and other tools enable educators to track valuable qualitative and quantitative data.

No matter the medium, communication is the pivotal element in positively applying assessment data. If used with care and intention, information pertinent to student progress creates an outline for teachers to have an open dialogue with their students about their goals, strengths, and areas needing improvement. Quality feedback in a timely manner is essential to maintaining the motivation and determination required to consistently attend class.

"Feedback is like a barometer we use to help us know whether or not we have understood something accurately or whether we are performing a new skill as intended. Without feedback, we only have our own perspective, which isn't always accurate. While we may not always like the feedback we receive, we typically crave knowing if we are on the right track."

—Dana Childress, Early Intervention
Strategies for Success

"Effective feedback plays a critical role in helping adult learners achieve their educational goals and reach their maximum potential. It should be an integral part of every adult education program."

—A K Sachdeva, National Library of Medicine

Despite the extreme value of quality feedback and tracking progress toward a goal, many actively avoid this exercise. It's human nature. We all want to feel the success and accolades of achievement. But few relish the process of evaluating strengths and weaknesses along the way. This is especially prominent in the adult student community as many already feel a sense of defeat or embarrassment for not completing high school in a traditional manner. Many students look at long-term markers such as passing the test, earning a credential, and getting the job as the sole indicator of success. But the statement "If I didn't pass, I failed" is rarely true.

As educators, we have the opportunity to shape this narrative. Our adult students need to understand that growth takes time. Even if they have not yet achieved their ultimate goal, their efforts matter. We explored this concept at length in Retention Anchor 3 as we discussed the power of a growth mindset. Assisting a student in tracking their progress provides a framework for a growth-oriented view of success. As they navigate their personal path, looking back becomes just as important as looking forward.

In exploring systems to track student progress at Bonny Eagle Adult Education, PLC educator Cherie Goranites notes, "Tracking how far you've come and seeing the difference in where you were compared to where you are, drives you forward." In her reflection, Goranites references the work of Omar Itani in his article, "The Power of Progress: Measure The Gain, Not The Gap." Itani writes, "The proper way of measuring progress? Look backward, not forward. Gaze from where you are today, back to where you were when you first started. Do you see all the progress you've made? That backward distance is defined as "The Gain," and it's much more inspiring, motivational, and rewarding than what

lies ahead in "The Gap." Adult educators must develop and utilize progress tracking that allows students to celebrate the gain versus fearing the gap. Program retention rests on the student's belief that there is a way forward. They just have to keep moving.

Celebrating Progress

If valuing progress over performance is the goal, we must consider how we celebrate growth. Humans are hard-wired for reward. Our brains are designed to crave incentives. We want the "gold star." We long for praise and recognition. We want something of substance to prove to ourselves and others that we did something meaningful.

The dilemma is that many big goals highlight the final reward and neglect small victories within the journey. If progress is to be honored, we must find ways to recognize forward movement, not just crossing the finish line. Acknowledging incremental progress will help students commit to attending class, persevere in the midst of struggle, and continue to work diligently in the classroom.

"By cataloging and celebrating our small wins each day, we can be reminded that we are making meaningful progress. And, in truth, it's the small wins [that] all add up to actually complete the big projects and big goals."

— Shawn Blanc, The Focus Course

"Not only does celebrating success feel good in the moment, but it also sets you up for future success. Taking the time to recognize your achievements allows you the chance to pinpoint exactly what worked so that you can repeat it in the future. Taking pride in your accomplishments by celebrating them—even the small ones—can also boost your self-confidence and motivate you to achieve more."

—Jodi Clarke, Verywell Mind

Brainstorming creative ways to celebrate adult student progress may seem challenging, but many approaches may be simpler than you think. We asked our PLC to research and share a few ways to honor student achievement en route to success. Here are some of their suggestions.

- **Verbal praise.** Provide specific, complementary feedback when possible. Telling students they did a "Great job" is nice. But noting a precise detail such as "I liked the way you worked hard to find the correct answer to this question" is more impactful.

- **Handwritten notes or cards.** A thoughtful expression of pride in a student goes a long way. Be specific about a direct achievement or gain.

- **Prize banks and treasure chests.** Adult students like candy and stickers too!

- **Displaying student work.** Students feel a greater sense of self-worth when their teachers and peers appreciate their work.

- **Certificates of achievement.** Create something simple but tangible that a student can hold and share that signifies a specific accomplishment.

- **Attendance recognition.** Highlight total hours of instruction to place special value on class attendance.

- **Character awards.** Recognize stand-out students with admirable qualities like resilience, punctuality, collaboration, communication, and responsibility.

- **Progress parties.** Devote a bit of class time to a small celebration to recognize milestone accomplishments.

- **Class challenges.** Set a group goal for students to work toward. Reward with a special game or shared treat.

Measuring, tracking, and celebrating student progress enables educators to set the stage for strong student retention and program completion. As students edge closer to their why, their commitment to achieving their goals is energized. As teachers facilitate student success, their dedication to adult education is strengthened. Student retention and teacher retention unite and prosper in environments that value feedback and use it intentionally to invoke change.

ACTIVITIES AND APPLICATIONS

To support you and your students in setting goals and tracking progress, we have created a customizable tool to guide conversations about immediate, short-term, midpoint, and long-term goals. Essential Education's *Goal Navigation Worksheet* (see below) prompts students to set a time-bound goal linked to a personal incentive. There are spaces to discuss what reaching each goal might require of the student and an open area for journaling and reflection. Be sure to include both quantitative and qualitative measures of progress. You can access the *Goal Navigation Worksheet* reproducible resource within the **Measuring Progress Webinar Handout** (see Appendix I). We've even provided a sample exercise for your reference.

Goal Navigation Worksheet: EXAMPLE

Complete the following information below.

Student: _Matty G._

Career Objective: _Graphic Designer_

Immediate Goal:	**Short-Term Goal:**	**Mid-Point Goal:**	**Long-Term Goal:**
	Improve GED Math PT		
Dividing Fractions	*Score by 5 pts*	*Pass GED Math PT*	*Pass GED Math*
Time Frame:	**Time Frame:**	**Time Frame:**	**Time Frame:**
			1/1 Ave 8/10 ques
Mastery by 11/1	*12/1*	*12/25*	*correct*
Effort:	**Effort:**	**Effort:**	**Effort:**
Mastery by 11/1	*Review previous test*	*Review Previous Test*	
ID needs	*ID Needs*	*Strengthen skills*	*Review score report*
Take a PT	*Take a PT*	*Review missed ques.*	*Review missed ques.*
Reward:	**Reward:**	**Reward:**	**Reward:**
Favorite treat	*Fun afternoon*	*Night out with friends*	*Celebration Dinner*

Goal Navigation Worksheet: EXAMPLE (cont.)

Complete the following information below.

Journey Journal:

11/1: Feel pretty good about fractions. Will continue to review.

12/1: Improved score by 7 points! Yay me!

12/25: Missed passing by 2 points. Bummed but I know what I need to do to pass. Will take another PT in a

week.

1/1: I passed! If I can pass math, I know I can pass my other subjects. Time to set some new goals!

*SMART GOAL Reminder: Specific, Measurable, Attainable, Realistic, Time-Bound

TOP TAKEAWAYS

Measuring Progress: Tracking, Improving, and Celebrating Gains

- *Student data is multifaceted.* Wise educators recognize the value of quantitative and qualitative measures of progress.

- *Multiple forms of assessment create a clearer picture of student success.* Varying indicators of growth provide teachers and administrators with a clearer picture of where adult students are, where they hope to go, and what type of support is required to get them there.

- *Student-friendly tracking tools improve motivation and engagement.* Adult learners need to know their efforts are paying off. They need to see the results of their labor in an easy to understand format.

- *Data-driven instruction is invaluable.* When adult educators use student data to customize instruction, they are better able to target individual strengths and needs.

- *All student gains should be celebrated.* Acknowledging incremental progress will help students commit to attending class, persevere through struggles, and continue to work diligently in the classroom.

ANCHOR CONNECTION

Use the following questions to note connections between Retention Anchors.

How is measuring student progress supported by the previously explored Retention Anchors?

How do the known characteristics of adult learners influence student progress?

How can Just-In-Time Learning impact the way students view personal progress?

How can a positive classroom culture support student growth?

How can strong classroom relationships aid in helping students embrace feedback?

In what ways might educator professional development impact measuring, tracking, and celebrating progress?

How is retention impacted by student growth?

SUPPORT FROM ESSENTIAL EDUCATION

Essential Education is here to support educator endeavors to build strong classroom connections that improve student retention. Our product features and program offerings assist in strengthening the communication and curiosity required to build healthy school-based relationships in the following ways:

Measurable Skill Gains Accelerator Handbooks: This collection of resources allows educators to gain a greater understanding of student educational functioning levels (EFL) and the exact skills needed to yield significant gains. Learn how to target the standards students need to advance in TABE, CASAS, and HSE programs.

Student Progress Report: The Student Progress Report provides a time-saving, comprehensive view of student performance. This highly visual report eliminates the need to review multiple complicated reports and data sources. By displaying critical markers of student progress, like student study time, skill gains, and skill gaps in one easy place, instructors enjoy a clear, consolidated view of each student's skill mastery and movement toward their goals.

Retention Anchor 5: Measuring Progress

GROWING PROFESSIONALLY

CONTINUING EDUCATION FOR PROGRAM RETENTION

REVIEWING THE RESEARCH

We've emphasized the importance of educator professional development in each Retention Anchor thus far. Continued education and instructor collaboration allow teachers and administrators to learn more about *who* students are, *what* will be taught, *where* learning will take place, *how* supportive connections can be established, and *why* systems to measure and track progress are vital to student motivation and continuance. As we reach our final Anchor in the series, let's focus on how building professional expertise and flexibility equips teachers to deliver engaging instruction *when* needed. Growing professionally is the "when" of the Retention Anchors.

Professional development in education (PD) has long been championed as one of the best ways to improve teacher effectiveness and student outcomes. Educators will experience a range of professional development opportunities throughout their careers. Some professional training will be mandated by programmatic requirements or state and national standards. Some may link directly to school grants and funding sources. Many teachers and administrators must obtain a certain number of PD hours to retain current certifications or advance in new educational roles. While there is a systematic nature to the structure of PD opportunities, the ultimate goal is to promote educational excellence and enhance student success.

"When professional development is done well, it provides an opportunity for teachers to grow their knowledge and sharpen their skills, which can lead to better student outcomes. It's a way for teachers to collaborate with their colleagues and one avenue through which administrators can support their teachers."

—Sarah Swartz, Education Week

> *"Effective professional development ensures that teachers at whatever level in their careers have opportunities to learn new skills and practices, better equipping them to support students."*

—The Partnership for the Future of Learning, Teaching Profession Playbook

In essence, professional development offerings seek to provide teachers with at-the-ready resources that enable them to pivot and meet the needs of students as they arise. In Retention Anchor 2, we highlighted the importance of this type of instructional agility in meeting the Just-In-Time Learning needs of diverse adult students. Educational preparedness and flexibility equip teachers with the tools needed to meet students in moments of clarity and capitalize on "Aha!" moments.

In addition to improving teaching techniques known to bolster student retention, professional development has also been linked to the retention of high-quality educators. As noted in Retention Anchor 4, teacher-teacher relationships formed through collaboration not only benefit students, but teachers thrive when supported by like-minded colleagues. When those connections combine with professional training and resources, the impact on all members of the learning community is enhanced. Teacher well-being is also known to be improved by opportunities to grow professionally, as educators feel a greater sense of support and encouragement when equipped to do their jobs with excellence.

> *"By providing professional development opportunities, you can retain teaching staff by ensuring that they are engaged, motivated, and resilient to stress while also attracting prospective teachers."*

—Engage Education

"Our students deserve to be supported by teams of teachers who are dedicated to their success and well-being. Teachers who trust each other and are committed to continuous professional growth."

—Debra Meyer, Elmhurst University

The variety in types of professional development for educators is abundant. Local workshops and training courses are the most common, but strides are being made to develop new, timely, and cost-effective options for quality PD resources. Consider the following.

Conferences and Seminars

Conference opportunities allow educators to step outside their typical teaching environment and learn from experts in the field. These opportunities also provide instructional teams time to learn and grow together, strengthening teacher-teacher bonds.

"Education conferences are great professional development opportunities. Not only will you learn about the latest innovations in your field, but you'll also have the chance to connect with other professionals from outside your school district or even your state."

—Suzanne Capek Tingley, Hey Teach!

Curriculum-Based Training

Instruction on how to best implement and use the program curriculum is extremely beneficial to educators. This training encourages good stewardship of program resources.

"Curriculum-based training is vital for teachers to understand what content will appear and what it will look like. Educators need to spend time reviewing content maps to see how topics are covered and where they are placed in the curriculum. This is especially important when blending online learning with in-class experiences."

—Charlie Weeks, Essential Education

Coaching and Peer Observation

Instructional coaches and fellow educators are terrific sources of mentorship and advising. Targeted peer observations and guided support can improve instruction and boost teacher morale.

> "A 2018 meta-analysis of 60 studies on instructional coaching found that it can improve teachers' practice, so much so that in some cases, a novice teacher performed at the same level as one who had been in the classroom for 5 years. It improves student performance, too, as measured by standardized test scores."
>
> —Sarah Swartz, Education Week

Collegiate Courses

Educators passionate about a certain subject or area of expertise may consider pursuing an advanced degree. These opportunities not only enhance knowledge and skill, they can lead to greater leadership opportunities and salary increases.

Professional Learning Communities (PLC)

We know first-hand about the power and effectiveness of a PLC. The learning community contributing to this guide has been an invaluable source of innovation and encouragement. Learning communities can be organized in a variety of ways to produce meaningful results. Some revolve around specific research topics, while others focus on a specific skill or area of instruction. PLC embodies the unified strength of quality resources and teacher collaboration.

> "PLCs are the lifeblood of innovation and risk-taking in school. When structured well, they can be teams that constantly learn together and work to discover what is best for students."
>
> —Andrew Miller, Edutopia

EVALUATION AND REFLECTION

Despite the many benefits of professional development for educators, there are obstacles and conditions that impede access to timely and effective PD resources. Of course, time and funding for training are common concerns. However, a larger debate exists when it comes to identifying what defines exemplary professional development.

Teacher PD, Explained

In a 2023 article published by Education Week, entitled "Teacher Professional Development, Explained," author Sarah Swartz reports that despite attempts at the national level to create standards for professional development offerings, most resources do not meet the suggested criteria. She writes, "Most professional development is locally provided, from school districts, regional offices of education, or teachers' unions. Quality control is often lacking: Some states have hundreds of approved providers and only audit a small sample each year" (Swartz, 2023).

So what are the federal guidelines for high-quality professional development? The *Every Student Succeeds Act* (ESSA) outlines these six key criteria. PD opportunities should be sustained, intensive, collaborative, job-embedded, data-driven, and classroom-focused.

- **Sustained.** For professional development initiatives to be effective, there must be a circular or repetitive nature to the training. One-off, singular sessions are rarely helpful for long-term application. Follow-up instruction and time to reflect on the implementation of new strategies yield more sustainable takeaways.

- **Intensive.** Targeting one specific instructional skill or standard increases efficiency. Additional studies show that focusing on practical classroom strategies has a stronger link to student performance than offerings solely focused on the teacher's knowledge of the subject matter.

- **Collaborative.** The power of teacher-teacher relationships is evident. Iron sharpens iron. When educators work together toward a common purpose, professional development is more efficient and uniquely contextualized by the contributions of multiple instructors.

- **Job-embedded.** Professional training is most effective when linked to practical application. The approach is sometimes called curriculum-based professional development and seeks to better utilize programs and systems already in place.

- **Data-driven.** Without information, alterations to classroom instruction are based purely on assumption. Quality data about student progress and instructional effectiveness turn reactionary changes into responsive strategies.

- **Classroom-focused.** The classroom is the beating heart of student success. The expectations, behavior patterns, academic culture, and personalized instruction cultivated in a learning environment can make or break a student's educational experience. Professional development geared to improve classroom endeavors is crucial.

Quality PD Opportunities

That's how the policymakers define effective PD in education. But do educators agree? What qualities do teachers deem the most important in professional development? A 2021 survey of over 8,000 educators conducted by the RAND Corporation solicited teacher thoughts on quality PD opportunities.

Let's examine the results of the 2021 RAND educator survey. Due to the diverse types of professional development offered, the educators surveyed expressed differing opinions influenced by personal experience and time spent in the field. However, common themes emerged when participants described their thoughts on effective professional development. Additionally, these opinions shared many similarities with the characteristics listed within ESSA guidelines. While the semantics may vary, the core principles have common ground.

Teachers want professional development to be:

- Reflective; allowing time for implementation, evaluation, and follow-up (Sustained)
- Tailored to real teacher needs and pain points (Intensive)
- Inclusive of time to reflect with colleagues (Collaborative)
- Practical and connected to their work (Job-Embedded)
- Up-to-date; based on current learning theory (Data-driven)
- Relevant to a specific subject area or skill (Classroom-focused)

Educators also noted they would like to see more training focused on applications for specific learning groups, including ESL, ESOL, and students with learning differences.

The collective agreement between the ESSA criteria and surveyed educator needs is extremely helpful for teachers and administrators in selecting, planning, and conducting professional development. Having these characteristics top of mind will guide and support any initiative to improve PD opportunities. More robust resources will equip teachers with the skills and support required to better meet diverse student needs and assist adult learners in continuing their path to success.

Quick Reflection

Before reading the survey responses, write down a few ideas of your own. Do you agree with the ESSA suggested criteria? What do you think are the most significant characteristics of quality professional development?

Quick Reflection

After reading through both sets of quality PD characteristics and noting the similarities, which element(s) do you think has a greater impact on student retention? Is any one facet more apt to help students remain in class? Or do they all work together to support student engagement and continuance?

ACTIVITIES AND APPLICATIONS

Essential Education is dedicated to supporting adult educators in their efforts to change lives through learning. With that commitment in mind, we've created the **Professional Development Notetaking Guide** (see Appendix J) to help teachers and administrators make the most of any professional development opportunity made available to them. Using the research provided by ESSA and the RAND Corporation, this resource walks educators through questions and reflections aligned to characteristics associated with high-quality professional development. Use this guide for an upcoming training or PD session. We trust it will provide greater planning, reflection, and application of educational research and resources.

TOP TAKEAWAYS

Growing Professionally: Continuing Education for Program Retention

- *Teacher education and student performance are intertwined.* Professional Development (PD) in education has long been noted as one of the best ways to improve teacher effectiveness and student outcomes.

- *Professional development opportunities promote teacher continuance.* In addition to improving teaching techniques known to bolster student retention, PD has also been linked to the retention of high-quality educators.

- *The Every Student Succeeds Act (ESSA) outlines six key professional development criteria.* PD opportunities should be sustained, intensive, collaborative, job-embedded, data-driven, and classroom-focused.

- *Quality professional development is structured.* Effective PD involves planning, reflecting, and applying educational research and resources.

- *Educators need timely tools.* Providing robust resources will equip teachers with the skills and support required to better meet diverse student needs and assist adult learners in continuing their path to success.

ANCHOR CONNECTION

Use the following questions to note connections between the six Retention Anchors.

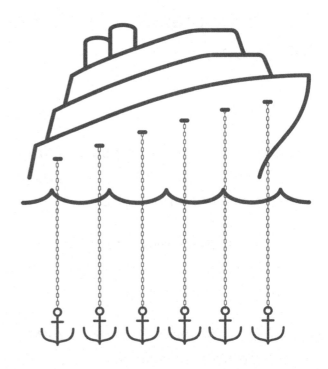

How does professional development impact the previously explored retention anchors?

How do the known characteristics of adult learners influence professional development?

How can Just-In-Time Learning be enhanced by professional development?

How can professional development support a positive classroom culture?

How can professional development improve student progress?

How does professional development impact retention?

SUPPORT FROM ESSENTIAL EDUCATION

The breadth and depth of Essential Education's professional development offerings are unmatched. Check out a few of our most popular courses and learning resources.

Professional Development Series. Three online courses designed specifically for the adult education instructor. Teachers are able to view their progress, participation time, and lesson mastery in easy-to-read charts located on their learning dashboard. Administrators have the ability to assign specific courses and track them in the built-in Learning Management System (LMS). The courses include Identifying and Remediating Reading Skills Difficulties, Motivating the Adult Learner, and Blended Learning in Adult Education. Visit https://bit.ly/3uwPbgJ.

Distance Learning Series. Six free downloadable courses created in partnership with real-life distance learning educators. Starting with the basics and moving to more advanced, this series touches on some of the most common distance learning topics in adult education. Each course will provide valuable ideas, tools, and resources to immediately implement in a virtual classroom. Visit https://bit.ly/3uuTLMu.

Teacher Toolkit. A variety of free resources aimed at helping educators keep their students engaged in a hybrid classroom. From professional development and tutorial videos to instructional guides and templates, this toolkit will help educators create an engaging hybrid classroom, understand popular technology tools, implement Essential Education products, and recruit new students. Visit https://bit.ly/3sWTykX.

Tuesdays with Essential Education (TWEED). Free live webinars discussing the latest topics, teaching strategies, and trends in adult education. All attendees receive recap materials at the conclusion of each webinar, including a Certificate of Participation, a recording of the webinar, and the presentation deck. Visit https://bit.ly/49TKMor.

Teaching for Improvement & Program Success (TIPS). Free live webinars focusing on different topics within the Adult Education field, showing instructors how to use our LMS to overcome common problems, accelerate learning, and accomplish their various classroom goals. Hosted by Essential Education's Educator Support Team to ensure all instructors are up to speed and using Essential Education to their benefit. Visit https://bit.ly/46AAzKN.

ANCHOR
SUMMATION
THE SIX ANCHORS OF
ADULT STUDENT RETENTION

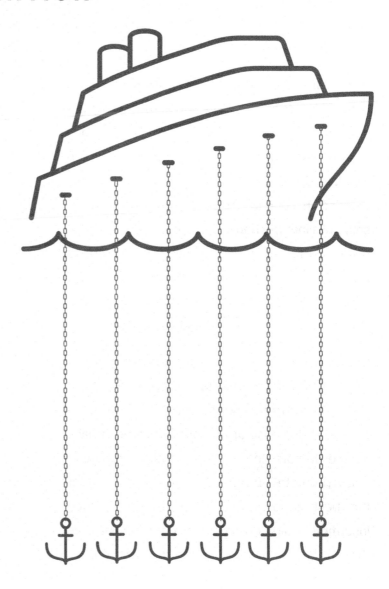

In having a deep understanding of who students are (see Anchor 1, page 5), we are better able to plan what we teach (see Anchor 2, page 23) to meet the just-in-time needs of adult learners. In helping students take their next steps toward success, we consider where learning will occur (see Anchor 3, page 43) and strive to build a culture that promotes progress and encourages students to pursue their why (see Anchor 4, page 81). After exploring how positive interactions shape the classroom (see Anchor 5, page 109), we foster a learning environment that motivates students to connect with their peers and teachers to collaborate with each other. As we grow professionally, we sharpen tools to assist students when they need support (see Anchor 6, page 129).

Like many big problems, the issue of adult student retention cannot be solved with a singular solution. There isn't a magic pill, instantaneous fix, or quick remedy. Anchoring student retention requires the collective force of multiple factors working in concert. As the proverbial retention ship pulls into the harbor, each anchor is crucial in securing the vessel. Storms will come, and tides will rise and fall. At some point, one anchor may bear more weight than the others. However, core stability is found in their collective strength.

But here's the thing about anchors. They aren't nets. They cannot provide protection for items lost in the ebb and flow of the sea. They are not a catch-all but a base of support. The same applies to the factors that anchor student retention and promote program completion. Under the best conditions, some learners will face insurmountable obstacles and circumstances that impede continuance. Even the most caring, equipped educators may be unable to remove all of the success barriers adult students face.

Still, we must press on, remain vigilant, and stand in the gap for those we have the honor to serve. Whether for a brief moment or an enduring season, adult educators champion the cause of millions needing academic support. The Retention Anchors are foundational tools to bolster that mission. Our students need us. They need our support to keep trying, learning, and growing. They need us to continue to strengthen the elements we know will help keep them motivated and engaged.

So let's continue the conversation. Let's continue the hard work. Let's continue to question, investigate, and evaluate. Let's continue to find innovative solutions to promote progress. We are better together, and our collaborative efforts can revolutionize adult student retention and change lives through education.

ACKNOWLEDGEMENTS

Author's Letter

Dear 2023 Essential Education Professional Learning Community,

Words fail to convey the sincere appreciation we have for the countless contributions you have made to our year-long exploration of adult student retention. The dedication and support you have given to this initiative and to each other cannot be quantified. Your questions, in-depth research, classroom experiments, and deeply personal reflections have been invaluable. Without them, this venture would not have been possible.

Throughout our time together, many of you faced and persevered through personal and professional struggles. Your resilience is exemplary, and your commitment to your students is extraordinary. It is beyond encouraging to see the level of excellence and care each of you brings to the field of adult education. Take heart in knowing your efforts are making a difference as we continue to "show up for the ones that show up."

We trust this experience has been as meaningful to you as it has been for our team at Essential Education. We covet your continued support and collaboration as partners and friends. The work we do is not easy, but worthwhile endeavors rarely are.

With heartfelt gratitude and acknowledgment of a job well done, we thank you.

Jen Denton

Jen Denton
Director of Educational Development
 essential education

Additional appreciation to Dan Griffith, whose valuable contributions to the 2023 Professional Learning Community and its retention initiatives will continue to support and equip adult educators for years to come.

Special thanks to our partners at the Coalition on Adult Basic Education (COABE) for supporting Essential Education's 2023 Professional Learning Community. Your certification of members completing the Retention Specialist Program is invaluable. Thank you for celebrating the outstanding efforts of teachers and administrators working to build thriving adult education programs.

COABE Certified Retention Specialists

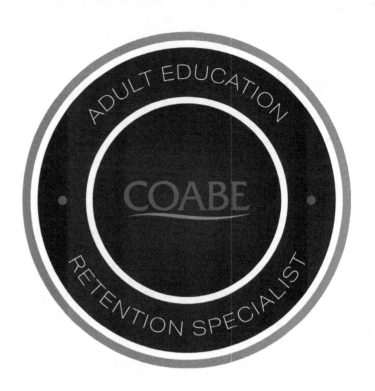

Bilquis Ahmed
Instructional Lead Teacher
South Bay Adult School
bahmed@rbusd.org

Dr. the Hon. D. Neletha Butterfield, M.B.E., J.P., Ed. D
Director
C.A.R.E. Learning Centre
carelearning83@gmail.com

Ester Garcia
GED Instructor
Catholic Charities Adult Education Center
mse.ged.clc@gmail.com

Cherie Goranites
Academic Coordinator
Bonny Eagle Adult Education
cgoranites@bonnyeagle.org

Kelly Grudowski
Site Director
Orion Education and Training
kgrudowski@orioneducation.org

Chaw Kalayar
ERA Program Coordinator
Prince George's Community College
kalayacx@pgcc.edu

Tracy Reid
Tutoring Lab Coordinator
SUNY Syracuse Educational Opportunity Center
reidts@morrisville.edu

Lyle Ring
Adult Education Lead Teacher
Briya Public Charter School
lring@briya.org

Christina Smith
Adult Education Instructor
Goodwill Gulf Coast
csmith@goodwillgc.org

Susan Spradlin
Virtual Lead Instructor
Tennessee College of Applied Technology
susan.spradlin@tcatknoxville.edu

LaDonna Torrey, M.S.Ed. CALT
GED Educator
Hutchinson Community College
ABE/Corrections
torreyl@hutchcc.edu

Tammy Zirkle
ISAEP/Computer Mathematics Teacher
Waynesboro Public High School
tzirkle@waynesboro.k12.va.us

RESOURCES

American University School of Education. (2020, July 23). Qualitative vs. quantitative research: Comparing the methods and strategies for education research. https://soeonline.american.edu/blog/qualitative-vs-quantitative/

American University School of Education. (2020, December 10). How to foster a growth mindset in the classroom. https://soeonline.american.edu/blog/growth-mindset-in-the-classroom/

Atkins, M. (2022, April 20). 15+ Strategies to help with student accountability. BetterLesson. https://betterlesson.com/blog/strategies-student-accountability

Badaracco, J. L. (2020). Step back: Bringing the art of reflection into your busy life. Harvard Business Review Press.

Blanc, S. (2015, January 30). Recognize and celebrate your progress. The Focus Course. https://thefocuscourse.com/celebrate-progress/

Bouchrika, I. (n.d.). Teacher collaboration guide: Strategies, statistics & benefits. Research.com. https://research.com/education/teacher-collaboration-guide

California Academy of Sciences. (n.d.). What are norms and why do they matter? https://www.calacademy.org/what-are-norms-and-why-do-they-matter

Carol Dweck: A summary of the two mindsets. (n.d.). Farnam Street. https://fs.blog/carol-dweck-mindset/

Childress, D. (2015, June 24). Adult Learning Principle #5 – Feedback is How We Grow. Early Intervention Strategies for Success. https://www.veipd.org/earlyintervention/2015/06/24/adult-learning-principle-5-feedback-is-how-we-grow/

Cornell University. (n.d.). Collaborative learning. Center for Teaching Innovation. https://teaching.cornell.edu/teaching-resources/active-collaborative-learning/collaborative-learning

Deshpande, H. (n.d.). Examples of qualitative data in education: How to use. QuestionPro. https://www.questionpro.com/blog/examples-of-qualitative-data-in-education/

DeSteno, D., & Clarke, J. (2021, October 7). Healthy ways to celebrate success. Verywell Mind. https://www.verywellmind.com/healthy-ways-to-celebrate-success-4163887

Ehiemere, F. I. (2022, October). The role of evaluation in teaching and learning process in education. International Journal of Advanced Academic and Educational Research, 13(5). https://arcnjournals.org/images/2726145223713511.pdf

Elmore, T. (2021). The eight paradoxes of great leadership: Embracing the conflicting demands of Today's Workplace. HarperCollins Leadership.

Encalade, L. (2021, November 8). Two steps to build a resilient and positive school culture – Right now. National Institute for Excellence in Teaching. https://www.niet.org/newsroom/show/blog/steps-to-build-resilient-positive-school-culture

Engage Education. (2021, May 17). Why is professional development important for teacher retention? https://engage-education.com/blog/why-is-professional-development-important-for-teacher-retention/

Falasca, M. (2011, November). Barriers to adult learning: Bridging the gap. Australian Journal of Adult Learning, 51(3). https://files.eric.ed.gov/fulltext/EJ954482.pdf

Fletcher, J. (2023, June 2). 5 effective ways to support teacher collaboration. Edutopia. https://www.edutopia.org/article/5-effective-ways-support-teacher-collaboration

Fostering positive peer relationships. (n.d.). Transforming Education. https://transformingeducation.org/resources/fostering-positive-peer-relationships/

Galbraith, M. W. (Ed.). (1990). Adult learning methods: A guide for effective instruction. Krieger Publishing Company.

Greater Good in Education. (n.d.). Positive staff relationships. https://ggie.berkeley.edu/school-relationships/positive-staff-relationships/

HCL Jigsaw. (n.d.). 21st century skills: Why is problem-solving the need of the hour for school students? https://hcljigsaw.com/21st-century-skills-why-is-problem-solving-the-need-of-the-hour-for-school-students/

Indeed Editorial Team. (2021, April 23). 3 examples of great organizational culture — And how to develop it. Indeed. https://www.indeed.com/lead/build-great-organizational-culture

Innovare.(2023, September 17). Using qualitative data in education for better student outcomes. https://innovaresip.com/resources/blog/qualitative-data-in-education-student-outcomes/

Itani, O. (2021, August 15). The power of progress: Measure the gain, not the gap. OMAR ITANI. https://www.omaritani.com/blog/measure-progress-and-the-gain

Meador, D. (2019, July 22). The importance of effective communication between teachers. ThoughtCo. https://www.thoughtco.com/the-importance-of-effective-teacher-to-teacher-communication3194691

Miller, A. (2020, January 3). Creating Effective Professional Learning Communities. Edutopia. https://www.edutopia.org/article/creating-effective-professional-learning-communities/

The Ohio State University. (n.d.). Shaping a positive learning environment. Teaching and Learning Resource Center. https://teaching.resources.osu.edu/teaching-topics/shaping-positive-learning

Pappas, C. (2013, May 8). 8 important characteristics of adult learners. eLearning Industry. https://elearningindustry.com/8-important-characteristics-of-adult-learners

Pappas, C. (2017, December 29). 10 adult learning facts and stats that eLearning pros need to know. eLearning Industry. https://elearningindustry.com/adult-learning-facts-stats-elearning-pros-need-know

The Partnership for the Future of Learning. (2021, April 7). Chapter 3: Effective retention strategies. Teaching Profession Playbook. https://www.teachingplaybook.org/digital/chapter-3-retention

Portillo, J. (2020, June 16). Teacher retention: How to keep the best from leaving. Elmhurst University. https://www.elmhurst.edu/blog/teacher-retention/

Pourron, A. (n.d.). 10 Steps to build a successful company culture. LumApps. https://www.lumapps.com/employee-experience/how-to-build-company-culture/

Prothero, A. (2020, October 13). The essential traits of a positive school climate. Education Week. https://www.edweek.org/leadership/the-essential-traits-of-a-positive-school-climate/2020/10

Puiu, T., & Knowles, M. (2023, May 24). Adult learning theories: Unlocking the power of lifelong learning. ZME Science. https://www.zmescience.com/feature-post/resources/school-study/adult-learning-theories/

Sachdeva A. K. (1996). Use of effective feedback to facilitate adult learning. Journal of Cancer Education : The Official Journal of the American Association for Cancer Education, 11(2), 106–118. https://pubmed.ncbi.nlm.nih.gov/8793652/

Saka, O. A. (2021, January). Can teacher collaboration improve students' academic achievement in junior secondary mathematics? Asian Journal of University Education, 17(1). https://doi.org/10.24191/ajue.v17i1.8727

Scales, P. (2019, June 6). 'Sage on the stage' or 'guide on the side'. College Jobs. https://college.jobs.ac.uk/article/sage-on-the-stage-or-guide-on-the-side-/

Schwartz, S., & Ferlazzo, L. (2023, July 26). Teacher professional development, explained. Education Week. https://www.edweek.org/teaching-learning/teacher-professional-development-explained/2023/07

Stevens, E. (2023, May 11). What is quantitative data? CareerFoundry. https://careerfoundry.com/en/blog/data-analytics/what-is-quantitative-data/

Tingley, S. C. (n.d.). Education conferences are a great place for teachers to grow. Western Governors University. https://www.wgu.edu/heyteach/article/education-conferences-are-great-place-teachers grow1805.html

University of Missouri. (2022, March 7). Positive teacher-student relationships lead to better teaching. College of Education & Human Development. https://education.missouri.edu/2022/03/positive-teacher-student-relationships-lead-to-better-teaching/

University of Waterloo. (n.d.). Teaching problem-solving skills. Centre for Teaching Excellence. https://uwaterloo.ca/centre-for-teaching-excellence/catalogs/tip-sheets/teaching-problem-solving-skills

Valamis. (2023, June 15). 8 adult learning principles. https://www.valamis.com/hub/adult-learning-principles#life-experience

Veroff, D. (n.d.). "What you can learn about your community from demographics." https://leadershipdevelopment.extension.wisc.edu/articles/what-you-can-learn-about-your-community-from-demographics/

Voyager Sopris Learning. (2023, March 17). What are evidence-based practices in education? https://www.voyagersopris.com/vsl/blog/what-are-evidence-based-practices-in-education

Waterford.org. (2019, April 29). Why strong teacher student relationships matter. https://www.waterford.org/education/teacher-student-relationships/

Western Governors University. (2020, July 17). What is the transformative learning theory? https://www.wgu.edu/blog/what-transformative-learning-theory2007.html#openSubscriberModal

Wilton, P. (2018, April 26). Aha! moments linked to dopamine-producing regions in the brain. Goldsmiths, University of London. https://www.gold.ac.uk/news/aha-moment-dopamine/

APPENDIX

ATTENDANCE CHART, SOUTH BAY ADULT SCHOOL EXPERIMENT

Retention Anchor 1:
Knowing Your Audience: Who Is the Adult Student?

Do you know and understand what barriers the busy students in your program face?

Consider the activity performed at South Bay. The experiment used the following key to mark attendance and reasons for missing class. Use these or develop your own list with your class's input.

Use the following chart example as a reference to mark and measure student attendance. Allow for follow-up discussions and brainstorming of obstacle solutions.

MONTH

Attendance chart for Students 1–12 across days 1–30.

Legend

- ● PRESENT
- ○ SICK
- ○ TRANSPORTATION
- ○ CHILDCARE
- ○ WORK
- ● APPOINTMENT
- ● PERSONAL
- ? UNKNOWN

MONTH:

Name   1   2   3   4   5   6   7   8   9   10   11   12   13   14   15   16   17   18   19   20   21   22   23   24   25   26   27   28   29   30   31

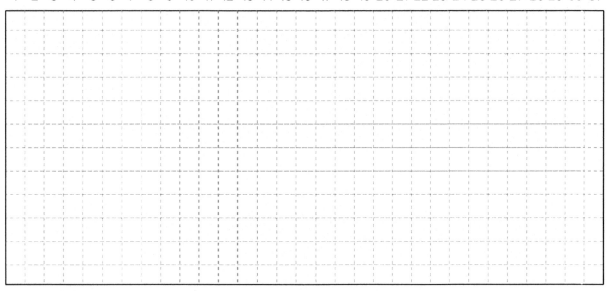

Legend

PRESENT

SICK

TRANSPORTATION

CHILDCARE

WORK

APPOINTMENT

PERSONAL

UNKNOWN

ONLINE STUDENT RESPONSE SURVEY, BRIYA PUBLIC CHARTER SCHOOL EXPERIMENT

Retention Anchor 1:
Knowing Your Audience: Who Is the Adult Student?

Approximately how long have you studied English in a classroom setting?

- ☐ Less than 6 months
- ☐ 6 months to 1 year
- ☐ 1 to 2 years
- ☐ More than 2 years

Approximately how long have you studied English at Briya Public Charter School?

- ☐ Less than 6 months
- ☐ 6 months to 1 year
- ☐ 1 to 2 years
- ☐ More than 2 years

Read over the following statements and indicate how much you agree or disagree with each one.

	Strongly Disagree	Disagree	Unsure	Agree	Strongly Agree
With enough hard work and time, I will reach my educational goals.					
I have a definite education or career goal that I am working toward.					
My family motivates me to continue studying English.					
Better English will likely help me obtain a better job in the future.					
Briya having a student service team has helped me stay in school this past year.					
The increased use of online classes and technology has helped me stay enrolled in school.					
I have considered dropping out of school because of technical issues in the past year.					
Without childcare, I could not be enrolled in English classes.					
My work situation has made it hard to attend classes.					
My family has made it hard to attend classes as much as I would like.					
I have considered dropping out of school in the past year					

In your own words, what motivates you to learn English and continue coming to class?

In your own words, what currently or in the past has made staying in class difficult for you?

STUDENT SURVEY TEMPLATE

Retention Anchor 1:
Knowing Your Audience: Who Is the Adult Student?

Rate the following statements and indicate how much you agree or disagree with each one.

	Strongly Disagree	Disagree	Unsure	Agree	Strongly Agree
I have a specific goal I want to achieve.					
I am motivated to succeed.					
I have the skills I need to succeed.					
I know I WILL succeed.					
I know how to manage my time.					
I enjoy learning.					
I know how I learn best.					
I enjoy working by myself.					
I enjoy working in groups.					
I get frustrated easily.					
I know how to check my progress.					
I feel comfortable asking questions.					

In addition to attending class, what activities and responsibilities require your time and attention? Check all that apply.

☐ Work (one job)

☐ Work (multiple jobs)

☐ Childcare

☐ Care for a family member

☐ Self-care (health issues, medical appts., etc.)

☐ Hobbies or volunteer activities

☐ Other:_____

Which of the following is a direct conflict or makes it hard to attend class? Check all that apply.

☐ Work

☐ Child/Family Care

☐ Transportation

☐ Financial factors

☐ Technology barriers

☐ Other:_____

Student Survey Template (cont.)

Why did you enroll in the program?

☐ To improve my education

☐ To prepare for a new or better job

☐ To fulfill a requirement

☐ Other:_____

What or who encourages you to achieve your goals? Check all that apply.

☐ Friends or Family: I want to make them proud.

☐ Me: I want to make myself proud.

☐ Money: I want to have financial stability.

☐ Education: I want to go to college.

☐ Career: I need to build the skills required to succeed in work.

☐ Other:_____

Have you attended other adult education programs in the past? If yes, why didn't you complete that program?

Do you have a specific career or education goal? If yes, what is it?

What would you like your teacher to know about you?

SCORING ACTIVITY TEMPLATE

Retention Anchor 2:
Capitalizing on the Now: Applying Just-In-Time Learning

Complete the chart below and "score" yourself on how prepared you are to give examples related to your students' goals or interests.

Student	Key Learning Needs	Key Goals/Interests	How prepared am I to give examples from this field? (1 = low, 10=high)
Ex: John Doe	Math basics	Welding, automotive design	

INDEPENDENT CULTURE WORKSHOP

Retention Anchor 3:
Creating Culture: Fostering an Environment for Student Success

Culture Checklist:

Select 3 characteristics* of your ideal classroom culture below.
*When describing your class, these are the 3 things you want to be evident.

- [ ] Collaborative
- [ ] Empathetic
- [ ] Innovative
- [ ] Motivating
- [ ] Casual

- [ ] Autonomous
- [ ] Inclusive
- [ ] Productive
- [ ] Encouraging
- [ ] Flexible

- [ ] Friendly
- [ ] Open
- [ ] Safe
- [ ] Supportive
- [ ] Fun

- [ ] Compassionate
- [ ] Authentic
- [ ] Competitive
- [ ] Enjoyable
- [ ] Enlightening

- [ ] Stimulating
- [ ] Inspirational
- [ ] Growth-oriented
- [ ] Understanding
- [ ] Meaningful

In your own words, define your top 3 cultural traits. What does this characteristic look like?

1.

2.

3.

Culture Evaluation:

Rate* the following statements below.
*Administrators should answer from a programmatic perspective.

My classroom is a safe space.

Definitely, yes!   Kind of   Not so much   Not at all

My classroom has clearly defined academic expectations.

Definitely, yes!   Kind of   Not so much   Not at all

My classroom has clearly defined expectations regarding classroom interactions.

Definitely, yes!   Kind of   Not so much   Not at all

My classroom is physically structured to support ideal culture.

Definitely, yes!   Kind of   Not so much   Not at all

Culture Evaluation (cont.):

My classroom models and welcomes valuable feedback.

| Definitely, yes! | Kind of | Not so much | Not at all |

My classroom implements evaluation-based strategies.

| Definitely, yes! | Kind of | Not so much | Not at all |

I recognize the life demands of my students.

| Definitely, yes! | Kind of | Not so much | Not at all |

I know my students' personal goals.

| Definitely, yes! | Kind of | Not so much | Not at all |

My classroom celebrates student achievement.

| Definitely, yes! | Kind of | Not so much | Not at all |

My classroom values effort.

| Definitely, yes! | Kind of | Not so much | Not at all |

Culture Check-In:

Rate* the following statements below.
To be administered to students.

I feel comfortable asking my teacher questions.

Definitely, yes!   Kind of   Not so much   Not at all

I feel comfortable asking my classmates questions.

Definitely, yes!   Kind of   Not so much   Not at all

I feel comfortable sharing ideas and opinions in my classroom.

Definitely, yes!   Kind of   Not so much   Not at all

I would describe my classroom as a safe space.

Definitely, yes!   Kind of   Not so much   Not at all

Homework and assignments: I understand what is expected of me.

Definitely, yes!   Kind of   Not so much   Not at all

Classroom interactions: I understand what is expected of me.

Definitely, yes!   Kind of   Not so much   Not at all

I always know how I am doing in my studies.

Definitely, yes!   Kind of   Not so much   Not at all

I feel comfortable discussing my work with my teacher.

Definitely, yes!   Kind of   Not so much   Not at all

I feel comfortable discussing my work with other students.

Definitely, yes!   Kind of   Not so much   Not at all

I know what I need to do to make progress.

Definitely, yes!   Kind of   Not so much   Not at all

My teacher knows my life demands outside of class.

Definitely, yes!   Kind of   Not so much   Not at all

My teacher understands my life demands outside of class.

Definitely, yes!   Kind of   Not so much   Not at all

Culture Check-In (cont.):

My teacher knows my personal goals.

Definitely, yes!   Kind of   Not so much   Not at all

Answer the following questions below.

What are 3 words to describe the perfect classroom?

[   ]

What are 3 words to describe your current classroom?

[   ]

Thinking about the statements above, would you like to share anything else?

[   ]

ALL ABOUT ME EXERCISE TEMPLATE

Retention Anchor 4:
Getting Connected: Creating Relationships for Continuance

All About Me:

Complete the following information below.

Name: _____

My friends call me: _____

Age: _____

Birthday *(month and day)*: _____

My family *(check all that apply)*:

☐ Spouse/significant other

☐ Children   ☐ Son(s)   ☐ Daughter(s)

☐ Grandkids   ☐ Grandson(s)   ☐ Granddaughter(s)

☐ Sibilings   ☐ Brother(s)   ☐ Sister(s)

# of pets: _____

What kind *(cat, dogs, lizard, etc.)*: _____

Three words that describe me:

1. _____

2. _____

3. _____

I am:

☐ an early bird

☐ a night owl

These are my favorite things:

Color: _____   Food: _____

Candy: _____   Hobby: _____

Holiday: _____   Music/band/musician: _____

TV show/movie: _____   Sport/team/athlete: _____

All About Me (cont.):

Something on my bucket list: _____

Three things I am most thankful for:

1. _____

2. _____

3. _____

About Why I Am Here:

I left traditional school because:

_____

_____

_____

I want my GED because:

_____

_____

_____

    The subject I enjoy the most is: _____

    The subject I struggle with is: _____

My biggest goal is:

_____

_____

_____

My dream job: _____

What/who motivates me: _____

What do I wish people (my classmates) knew about me?

_____

_____

_____

_____

STUDENT INFORMATION TABLE TEMPLATE

Retention Anchor 4:
Getting Connected: Creating Relationships for Continuance

Student Chart:

To be completed for incoming students.

Student's Name	Gender / Pronouns	Brief Description of Student's Educational Background	Goals	Learning Style *(Visual, Auditory, or Tactile)*	HA Math Practice Test Score	HA Reading Practice Test Score	HA Writing Practice Test Score

CURIOSITY = CONNECTION QUESTION GENERATOR

Retention Anchor 4:
Getting Connected: Creating Relationships for Continuance

Questions to Kickstart:

What's your favorite _____? What's your least favorite _____?

What kind of music/tv/movies/books do you like?

Where do you work?

What's for dinner?

What do you like to do when not working, studying, etc?

What are your 3 most used emojis?

What are you thankful for?

What's your why?

What/who motivates you?

What are your BIG goals?

Why did you leave traditional high school?

How would others describe you?

What do you wish people knew about you?

What's the most important quality for a teacher to have?

What can I do to support/encourage you?

Questions to Keep Going:

How's _____ going?

How are you feeling about _____?

How's your stress level? What do you do to cope?

What's been the hardest part of your week/month?

What do you want to accomplish this week/month?

Questions to Keep Going (cont.):

What did you learn this week/month?

What's one thing you would do differently this week/month?

What's your biggest obstacle right now?

What's been your biggest win this week/month?

How did that make you feel?

What can I do to support/encourage you?

Questions to Keep Up:

What's the biggest challenge you've overcome?

What are you most proud of?

What would you say to yourself 6 months/1 year ago?

What have you learned about yourself?

How do you define success?

What's next?

What do you need to get there?

What can I do to support/encourage you?

MEASURING PROGRESS WEBINAR HANDOUT

Retention Anchor 5:
Measuring Progress: Tracking, Improving, and Celebrating Gains

Adult education participants make measurable skill gains.

Measurable skill gains (MSG) demonstrate participants' progress toward achieving a credential or employment. MSGs are reported for all participants in adult basic education (ABE), adult secondary education (ASE) and English as a second language (ESL) programs. In program year 2020–21, **35% of adult education participants made a measurable skill gain.** Measurable skill gain numbers were impacted by COVID-19.

Participants with MSG

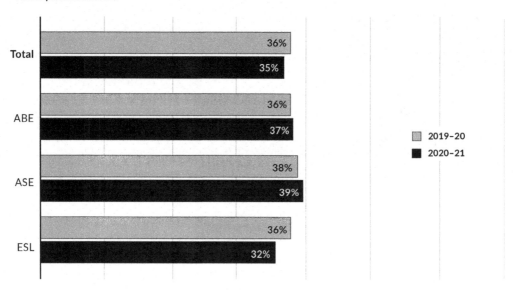

Participants can demonstrate MSG in two ways: educational functioning level (EFL) gain and receipt of a secondary school diploma.

In program year **2020–21:**

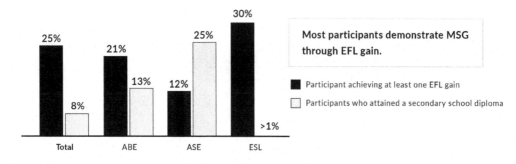

National Reporting System Learning Level Overview

NRS Level 1/2
Beginning ABE Literacy & Basic Education
Grade level 0 - 3.9

Reading & Writing

- Minimal reading and writing skills.

- May be able to read simple material on familiar subjects.

- May be able to write simple notes and messages on familiar situations.

- Little or no understanding of how print corresponds to spoken language.

- Have frequent errors in spelling.

Math

- Little or no recognition of numbers or simple counting skills.

- Minimal skills, such as the ability to add or subtract single-digit numbers, identify simple fractions, and work simple operations.

Job Skills

- Minimal knowledge of computers and related technology.

- Can provide limited personal information on simple forms.

- Can handle routine entry-level jobs that require little or no basic written communication and require minimal literacy skills.

National Reporting System Learning Level Overview (cont.)

NRS Level 3

Low Intermediate Basic Education

Grade Equivalent 4 - 5.9

Reading & Writing

- Can read simple texts with clear main ideas and structure.

- Can use context to determine meaning.

- Can interpret actions required in specific directions.

- Can write simple paragraphs with a main idea and supporting details on familiar topics.

- Can self and peer edit spelling and punctuation errors.

Math

- Can perform all four basic math operations using whole numbers up to three digits.

- Can identify and use all basic mathematical symbols.

Job Skills

- Can handle basic reading, writing, and computational tasks related to life.

- Can complete medical forms, order forms, or job applications.

- Can read simple charts, graphs, labels, and payroll stubs.

- Can use simple programs and complete basic tech tasks.

- Can qualify for entry-level jobs that require following basic written instructions with some clarification and assistance.

- Can write short reports and messages.

- Can read simple dials and scales and take routine measurements.

National Reporting System Learning Level Overview (cont.)

NRS Level 4
High Intermediate Basic Education

Grade level 6 - 8.9

Reading & Writing

- Able to read simple descriptions and text on familiar subjects.

- Able to access new vocabulary.

- Able to make some simple inferences and compare and contrast information (inconsistent).

- Able to write simple narrative descriptions and short essays with basic punctuation but struggle with more complex grammar.

Math

- Able to perform all four basic math operations with whole numbers and fractions.

- Able to determine correct math operations for solving narrative math problems.

- Able to convert fractions to decimals, decimals to fractions, and work basic operations with fractions.

Job Skills

- Able to handle basic life skills tasks.

- Able to understand simple graphs, charts, and labels.

- Able to follow multi-step diagrams, read simple employee handbooks and payroll stubs.

- Able to complete forms such as a job application, and reconcile a bank statement.

- Able to perform jobs that involve following simple written instructions and diagrams.

- Able to read procedural texts where the information is supported by diagrams.

- Able to learn or work with most basic computer software.

National Reporting System Learning Level Overview (cont.)

NRS Level 5

Low-High Adult Secondary Education

Grade Equivalent 9 - 12.9

Reading & Writing

- Can comprehend expository writing and identify spelling, punctuation, and grammatical errors.
- Can comprehend a variety of materials on common topics.
- Developing the ability to interpret meaning and critically think through written material.
- Can compose multi-paragraph essays.
- Can listen to oral instructions and write an accurate summary.
- Can identify the main idea in reading selections.
- Is developing the ability to write cohesively with clearly expressed ideas.
- Can write in an organized manner with few mechanical errors.
- Can use complex sentences.

Math

- Can perform all basic math functions with whole numbers, decimals, and fractions.
- Can interpret and solve simple algebraic equations, tables, and graphs.
- Can create and use tables and graphs.
- Is developing the ability to make mathematical estimates of time and space.
- Is developing an understanding of geometry to measure angles, lines, and surfaces.

Job Skills

- Can use math in business transactions.
- Can follow simple multi-step directions and read common legal forms and manuals.
- Is developing comprehension of college-level materials and apprenticeship manuals.
- Can link information from texts, carts, and graphs.
- Can complete forms, applications, and resumes.
- Can perform jobs that require interpreting information and writing or explaining tasks to other workers.
- Can use most common computer applications and appropriately use new software and technology.
- Can evaluate new work situations and processes.
- Can work productively and collaboratively in groups.
- Is developing team leadership skills.

Goal Navigation Worksheet:

Complete the following information below.

Student: _____

Career Objective: _____

Immediate Goal:

_____

Time Frame:

_____

Effort:

_____

Reward:

_____

Short-Term Goal:

_____

Time Frame:

_____

Effort:

_____

Reward:

_____

Mid-Point Goal:

_____

Time Frame:

_____

Effort:

_____

Reward:

_____

Long-Term Goal:

_____

Time Frame:

_____

Effort:

_____

Reward:

_____

Journey Journal:

_____

_____

_____

_____

_____

_____

_____

_____

*SMART GOAL Reminder: Specific. Measurable, Attainable, Realistic, Time-Bound

Goal Navigation Worksheet: (EXAMPLE)

Complete the following information below.

Student: _Matty G._

Career Objective: _Graphic Designer_

Immediate Goal:	**Short-Term Goal:**	**Mid-Point Goal:**	**Long-Term Goal:**
Dividing Fractions	_Improve GED Math PT Score by 5 pts_	_Pass GED Math PT_	_Pass GED Math_
Time Frame:	**Time Frame:**	**Time Frame:**	**Time Frame:**
Mastery by 11/1	_12/1_	_12/25_	_1/1 Ave 8/10 ques correct_
Effort:	**Effort:**	**Effort:**	**Effort:**
Mastery by 11/1 _ID needs_ _Take a PT_	_Review previous test_ _ID Needs_ _Take a PT_	_Review Previous Test_ _Strengthen skills_ _Review missed ques._	_Review score report_ _Review missed ques._
Reward:	**Reward:**	**Reward:**	**Reward:**
Favorite treat	_Fun afternoon_	_Night out with friends_	_Celebration Dinner_

Journey Journal:

11/1: Feel pretty good about fractions. Will continue to review.

12/1: Improved score by 7 points! Yay me!

12/25: Missed passing by 2 points. Bummed but I know what I need to do to pass. Will take another PT in a week.

1/1: I passed! If I can pass math, I know I can pass my other subjects. Time to set some new goals!

*SMART GOAL Reminder: Specific, Measurable, Attainable, Realistic, Time-Bound

PROFESSIONAL DEVELOPMENT NOTETAKING GUIDE

Retention Anchor 6:
Growing Professionally: Continuing Education for Program Retention

Professional Development Title: _____

Presenter(s): _____

Session Date/Time: _____

Location: _____

Colleagues in Attendance: _____

Prepare Your Mind:

Why are you attending this session? What do you hope to learn?

```
```

What do you already know about this topic?

```
```

Which area of development do you hope this session will target?

☐ Classroom management

☐ Instructional planning

☐ Teaching strategies

☐ Distance/hybrid learning techniques

☐ Content knowledge

☐ Application for ESL/ESOL learners

☐ Approaches for learning differences

☐ Retention strategies

☐ Workforce strategies

Capture Your Thoughts From the Session:

Notes	Ideas / Thoughts / Impressions

Apply What You've Learned:

What were the three most important takeaways?

Did the session address the specific area of development you hoped to target? If so, how?

How could the information relayed be integrated to enhance your current approaches and techniques?

Apply What You've Learned (cont.):

How will you apply or build on what you learned?

What colleague do you need to share this with? How will you collaborate with your team to apply the key takeaways from this session?

What data or resources would be helpful to support your efforts to develop newly discovered strategies?

Dig Deeper

What resources were highlighted during the training that you'd like to review?

Are there other additional resources you'd like to explore to build on what you've learned?

Are there other learning opportunities (past or future) that relate to this session? How do the topics complement one another?

Evaluate

Did you implement new strategies or apply new knowledge based on this session? If so, what?

What were the results?

What did you learn?

Will you continue to address strategies related to this topic?

Based on this implementation, are there additional development areas you want to explore?

essentialed.com/educators/professional-development-series